SUSTAINING SUPPORT FOR SOPHOMORE STUDENTS

RESULTS FROM THE 2019 NATIONAL SURVEY OF SOPHOMORE-YEAR INITIATIVES

Catherine Hartman and Dallin George Young

NATIONAL RESOURCE CENTER

FIRST-YEAR EXPERIENCE® AND STUDENTS IN TRANSITION
UNIVERSITY OF SOUTH CAROLINA

Research Report No.

11

Cite as:

Hartman, C., & Young, D. G. (2021). *Sustaining support for sophomore students: Results from the 2019 National Survey of Sophomore-Year Initiatives.* University of South Carolina, National Resource Center for The First-Year Experience & Students in Transition.

ISBN: 978-1-942072-54-6
Library of Congress Control Number: 2021919055
Published by:
National Resource Center for The First-Year Experience® and Students in Transition
University of South Carolina
1728 College Street, Columbia, SC 29208
www.sc.edu/fye

Production Staff for the National Resource Center:
Project Manager: Jennifer Keup, Executive Director
Design and Production: Stephanie L. McFerrin, Graphic Artist
External Reviewers: Tamara Rury, University of New Hampshire;
                             Vanessa Harris, Claflin University;
                             Holly Martin, University of Notre Dame

About the Publisher

The National Resource Center for The First-Year Experience and Students in Transition was born out of the success of the University of South Carolina's much-honored University 101 course and a series of annual conferences focused on the freshman year experience. The momentum created by the educators attending these early conferences paved the way for the development of the National Resource Center, which was established at the University of South Carolina in 1986. As the National Resource Center broadened its focus to include other significant student transitions in higher education, it underwent several name changes, adopting the National Resource Center for The First-Year Experience and Students in Transition in 1998.

Today, the Center collaborates with its institutional partner, University 101 Programs, in pursuit of its mission to advance and support efforts to improve student learning and transitions into and through higher education. We achieve this mission by providing opportunities for the exchange of practical and scholarly information as well as the discussion of trends and issues in our field through convening conferences and other professional development events such as institutes, workshops, and online learning opportunities; publishing scholarly practice books, research reports, a peer-reviewed journal, electronic newsletters, and guides; generating, supporting, and disseminating research and scholarship; hosting visiting scholars; and maintaining several online channels for resource sharing and communication, including a dynamic website, listservs, and social media outlets.

The National Resource Center serves as the trusted expert, internationally recognized leader, and clearinghouse for scholarship, policy, and best practice for all postsecondary student transitions.

Institutional Home

The National Resource Center is located at the University of South Carolina's (UofSC) flagship campus in Columbia. Chartered in 1801, UofSC Columbia's mission is twofold: to establish and maintain excellence in its student population, faculty, academic programs, living and learning environment, technological infrastructure, library resources, research and scholarship, public and private support and endowment; and to enhance the industrial, economic, and cultural potential of the state. The Columbia campus offers 324 degree programs through its 15 degree-granting colleges and schools. In fiscal year 2020, faculty generated $279 million in funding for research, outreach, and training programs. UofSC is among the top tier of universities receiving Research and Community Engagement designations from the Carnegie Foundation.

Contents

Tables and Figures

Tables

Figures

Introduction

It has now been over two decades since the National Resource Center for The First-Year Experience and Students in Transition published its first monograph on supporting sophomore-year students, *Visible Solutions for Invisible Students: Helping Sophomores Succeed* (Schreiner & Pattengale, 2000). Since then, the national conversation around needs of students after the first year of college has expanded and has become an impetus for research focused on more nuanced understandings of these students and support initiatives. This report builds upon trends and presents findings from the 2019 National Survey of Sophomore-Year Initiatives (NSSYI) conducted by the National Resource Center. NSSYI aimed to gather institution-level data about efforts and initiatives of colleges and universities focused on providing support, with a specific focus on the sophomore year. The 2019 NSSYI was the fourth administration of the survey, with previous iterations occurring in 2005, 2008, and 2014.

Previous administrations of the NSSYI, as well as other research on sophomores (see Schreiner & Tobolowsky, 2018; Skipper, 2019; Young et al., 2015), continually point to the importance and institutional reliance on academic advising to support sophomore-year students. When students matriculate on any given campus, they do so with expectations, hopes, and aspirations for success. Through institutional messages provided during recruitment, admission, enrollment, and orientation, students may believe that their college or university can deliver on helping them achieve their goals. Students' expectations do not simply dissolve with the successful completion of a first semester's or first year's worth of classes; it is thus imperative that staff continue support beyond students' first year. Many institutional staff understand that connecting students to majors, career paths, and the sense of community on a campus are important concerns in the overall picture of student success (Hunter et al., 2009; Skipper, 2019). As such, a growing proportion of colleges and universities indicate that they are implementing programs specifically designed to help sophomores achieve, succeed, and thrive and that advising is a critical tool that institutions can use to work toward these objectives (Schreiner et al., 2020; Skipper, 2019; Young et al., 2015).

Persistence and retention to and beyond the second year continue to be outcomes and objectives that matter to institutions (31.2% of institutions participating in the 2019 NSSYI; Skipper, 2019). But barring circumstances outside the institution's and students' control, these outcomes tend to be by-products and, at our most optimistic, proxies that students are engaging, learning, and becoming members of a number of communities that will contribute to their ongoing success (Reason, 2009). Moreover, there is good reason to believe that the effective institutional focus on the first-year experience has simply served to postpone attrition into the second year (Schreiner & Tobolowsky, 2018). The importance of the sophomore year and goals associated with student success should be communicated to all associated offices on campus and with students (Schreiner et al., 2018). As such, one of our aims with this report is to share results from the 2019 NSSYI about institutional objectives for students in the sophomore year and to show how they are connected to institutional structures set up to help students succeed.

As we present the results from the 2019 NSSYI, we have made an intentional effort to disaggregate the findings by institutional characteristics (i.e., community college vs. four-year institution; public vs. private) to highlight the ways different institutions are responding to their students' needs. Moreover, in the discussion we explore how administrators, faculty, researchers, and other interested stakeholders might begin to develop a more nuanced view of supporting sophomores. It is our hope that after reviewing this report, practitioners and researchers may be equipped with a greater understanding of a national picture of the ways that institutions are organized to support the students on their campuses after the first year. We also intend for readers to gain a better understanding of the ways in which institutional efforts and initiatives can be better designed to be responsive based on differences in campus context, student backgrounds, and student needs.

Organization of the Report

This report is divided into two sections: (a) an overview of the 2019 NSSYI and (b) a discussion of the results, with a focus on implications for practice and future research. In addition, the appendices provide a list of the participating institutions, the survey questionnaire, and the frequency distributions of responses to the NSSYI, disaggregated by institutional characteristics (i.e., type, control, and size of undergraduate enrollment). The information and tables in this report provide useful points of departure for institutions looking for ways to create or restructure sophomore-year programs.

2019 National Survey of Sophomore-Year Initiatives: Examining Institutional Environments

In 2019, the National Resource Center for The First-Year Experience and Students in Transition administered the National Survey of Sophomore-Year Initiatives (NSSYI). The primary goal of NSSYI is to collect information about institutional initiatives and objectives associated with supporting students through their sophomore year at colleges and universities in the United States. The subsequent sections of this report present details about the survey instrument, participating institutions, and analyses conducted, followed by a report of the survey findings.

Survey Instrument

The NSSYI was previously administered in 2005, 2008, and 2014. The 2019 questionnaire focused on the following content areas: (a) institutional information, (b) institutional attention to the sophomore year, (c) current sophomore-year initiatives, (d) coordination of sophomore-year initiatives, (e) primary institutional initiatives, (f) students reached by primary initiatives, (g) characteristics of initiatives, (h) educationally effective practices, (i) administration of the primary initiative, and (j) assessment and evaluation. The 2019 NSSYI was distributed to campus staff who are involved in sophomore-year initiatives, including individuals who were identified on the 2017 National Survey on The First-Year Experience as knowledgeable and willing to be contacted about sophomore-year initiatives; chief academic officers (CAOs); chief executive officers (CEOs); and/or chief student affairs officers (CSAOs) at regionally accredited, Title IV-eligible, undergraduate-serving institutions of higher education. Participants were invited via email to complete the survey. Specifically, the invitation notified participants that the National Resource Center was conducting an administration of NSSYI and confirmed that the participant was the appropriate contact and representative who could accurately provide information about second-year programming; if the participant was not the most suitable contact, we requested that they provide us with information about the correct campus contact.

In total, 3,931 institutions were invited to participate. The first wave of recruitment included a group of contacts at 547 institutions who were identified to be holders of knowledge about initiatives aimed at supporting second-year student success. These contacts were gathered through previous research at the National Resource Center, primarily through the 2017 National Survey on The First-Year Experience. After an initial wave of recruitment and reminders distributed via email, invitations were sent in successive waves to individuals at additional institutions. Contact information from listings available in the Higher Education Directory was used to identify and invite individuals to participate in the survey, including chief academic officers ($n = 3,207$), chief executive officers ($n = 3,561$), and chief student affairs officers ($n = 2,748$). A final wave of reminders to encourage participation went out to all groups before the recruitment period ended. Responses from a total of 308 institutions provided information about attention to sophomore issues on campuses, indicating a 7.8% response rate.

Participating Institutions

Table 1 presents the sample of campuses responding to the 2019 NSSYI compared to a national profile of institutions in the United States. The percentages in the table show that four-year institutions are slightly overrepresented in the sample of respondents. The sample also includes a smaller proportion of campuses with 1,000 or fewer undergraduate students (14.3%) than the national percentage (38.4%). Finally, private, for-profit institutions were greatly underrepresented in the sample. Because of the small number of participating for-profit colleges and universities in the survey and recognizing that these institutions operate in unique ways with respect to their students, these responses were not included in comparisons based on institutional control.

Table 1

Comparison of Institutional Characteristics

Institutional characteristic	National percentage (*N* = 3,848)	Percentages of all campuses responding to 2019 NSSYI (*N* = 308)
Type		
Community college[a]	35.3	16.2
Four-year	64.7	83.8
Control		
Public	42.7	52.9
Private, not-for-profit	38.3	44.8
Private, for-profit	19.0	2.3
Undergraduate enrollment		
Fewer than 500 students	26.3	5.5
501–1,000 students	12.1	8.8
1,001–1,500 students	8.3	9.1
1,501–3,000 students	17.4	19.8
3,001–5,000 students	11.1	14.6
5,001–10,000 students	12.7	20.5
10,001–15,000 students	4.9	4.9
15,001–20,000 students	2.8	4.2
More than 20,000 students	4.3	12.7

Note. Figures for the national percentages are from the Integrated Postsecondary Education Data System (IPEDS) by the National Center for Education Statistics (2020).

[a]In IPEDS, these institutions are referred to as "two-year institutions." In an effort to stay current with research and practice related to institutional characteristics, we refer to these institutions as "community colleges" throughout this report.

Analyses

To better understand the initiatives and objectives used by institutions to promote sophomore student success, we conducted descriptive analyses of the data. Comprehensive frequency distributions and sample percentages for each reported item were tabulated in the aggregate (total) across institutional type, control, and size. We used the following objectives to guide our inquiry and organize the 2019 NSSYI results:

- paint a national portrait of practices related to the sophomore year;

- understand the characteristics of initiatives, programs, and services aimed directly at sophomores;

- examine academic advising for sophomores, including its associated objectives, reach, and aims; and

- provide practitioners, decision makers, researchers, and educators useful tools for program design and opportunities for interaction with students.

The subsequent sections of this report focus on results and survey questions that highlight the student learning environment and those structures that might have the most proximate impact on it. Frequencies for all responses to the 2019 NSSYI are available in Appendix C.

Institutional Attention to Sophomores

The 2019 NSSYI included a series of questions about efforts related to students' sophomore-year experiences, such as the services implemented by institutions and the objectives associated with these initiatives. Additional questions focused on the length of time these services had been in place and how these efforts were coordinated across campus, including how centralized sophomore-year initiatives are. Next, we report select results from the 2019 NSSYI to highlight objectives and initiatives associated with the sophomore year.

Objectives Identified for the Sophomore-Year Experience

Participating institutions were asked to identify any campuswide objectives designed specifically for sophomores (see Tables 2 and 3). Institutions could select all options that applied from a list of 27 objectives. The most frequently reported objective across institutional types (including community colleges and four-year schools) was career exploration and/or preparation (49.0%), followed by academic planning (41.6%). Other frequently reported efforts included academic success strategies (35.7%); persistence, retention, or third-year return rates (31.2%); connection with the institution or campus (29.2%); introduction to a major, discipline, or career path (29.2%); major exploration (27.6%); and student–faculty interaction (26.9%). Notably, 31.8% of institutions across sectors had not identified campuswide objectives specifically for the sophomore year. This tendency was more prevalent at the community colleges in the sample (42.0% reporting) than four-year schools (29.8% reporting).

As the tables illustrate, priorities differed across institutional types. At community colleges (see Table 2), the most frequently reported objective for sophomores was academic planning (40.0%), followed by career exploration and/or preparation (36.0%) and academic success strategies (22.0%). Other objectives identified by community colleges in the sample included analytical, critical-thinking, or problem-solving skills (18.0%) and persistence, retention, or third-year return rates (18.0%). At four-year institutions, the most frequently reported objective for sophomores was career exploration and/or preparation, with over half of participating institutions (51.6%) reporting this activity at their schools. Additional frequently reported objectives included academic planning (41.9%); academic success strategies (38.4%); persistence, retention, or third-year return rates (33.7%); connection with the institution or campus (32.2%); and major exploration (32.2%). Differences also existed between public and private institutions in the sample, as well (see Table 3). Private schools were more likely to have career exploration and/or preparation specifically for sophomores (52.2% private vs. 47.2% public). Student–faculty interaction specifically for sophomores was also more frequently reported at private institutions (28.3% private vs. 25.8% public), as was a common sophomore-year experience (23.2% private vs. 12.9% public).

Table 2

Campuswide Objectives for Sophomores Identified by Institutions by Institutional Type

| | Institutional type | | | | Difference |
| | Community college | | Four-year | | |
Institutional objective	Freq.	%	Freq.	%	(%)
Percentages larger for community colleges					
Our institution has not identified campuswide objectives specifically for the sophomore year	21	42.0	77	29.8	12.2
Other	8	16.0	30	11.6	4.4
Information literacy	5	10.0	21	8.1	1.9
Analytical, critical-thinking, or problem-solving skills	9	18.0	43	16.7	1.3
Percentages larger for four-year institutions					
Major exploration	2	4.0	83	32.2	28.2
Student–faculty interaction	5	10.0	78	30.2	20.2
Connection with the institution or campus	7	14.0	83	32.2	18.2
Knowledge of institution or campus resources and services	4	8.0	64	24.8	16.8
Graduate or professional school preparation (e.g., premed, pre-law)	0	0.0	43	16.7	16.7
Academic success strategies	11	22.0	99	38.4	16.4
Common sophomore-year experience	2	4.0	52	20.2	16.2
Introduction to a major, discipline, or career path	8	16.0	82	31.8	15.8
Persistence, retention, or third-year return rates	9	18.0	87	33.7	15.7
Career exploration and/or preparation	18	36.0	133	51.6	15.6
Civic engagement	3	6.0	53	20.5	14.5
Personal exploration or development	6	12.0	62	24.0	12.0
Health and wellness	3	6.0	46	17.8	11.8
Integrative and applied learning	1	2.0	33	12.8	10.8
Writing skills	4	8.0	39	15.1	7.1
Introduction to college-level academic expectations	2	4.0	28	10.9	6.9
Oral communication skills	5	10.0	38	14.7	4.7
Social support networks (e.g., friendships)	8	16.0	53	20.5	4.5
Discipline-specific knowledge	5	10.0	37	14.3	4.3
Introduction to the liberal arts	1	2.0	16	6.2	4.2
Project planning, teamwork, or management skills	3	6.0	21	8.1	2.1
Academic planning	20	40.0	108	41.9	1.9
Developmental education, remediation, and/or review	2	4.0	12	4.7	0.7
Intercultural competence, diversity skills, or engaging with different perspectives	8	16.0	43	16.7	0.7
Digital literacy	3	6.0	16	6.2	0.2
Total	50	100.0	258	100.0	0.0

Table 3

Campuswide Objectives for Sophomores Identified by Institutions by Institutional Control

| | Institutional control | | | | Difference |
| | Public | | Private | | |
Institutional objective	Freq.	%	Freq.	%	(%)
Percentages greater for public institutions					
Knowledge of institution or campus resources and services	41	25.2	25	18.1	7.1
Our institution has not identified campuswide objectives specifically for the sophomore year	56	34.4	40	29.0	5.4
Persistence, retention, or third-year return rates	54	33.1	40	29.0	4.1
Social support networks (e.g., friendships)	35	21.5	24	17.4	4.1
Other	23	14.1	14	10.1	4.0
Introduction to college-level academic expectations	17	10.4	10	7.2	3.2
Academic planning	69	42.3	55	39.9	2.4
Information literacy	14	8.6	9	6.5	2.1
Introduction to a major, discipline, or career path	48	29.4	39	28.3	1.1
Civic engagement	31	19.0	25	18.1	0.9
Graduate or professional school preparation (e.g., premed, pre-law)	24	14.7	19	13.8	0.9
Academic success strategies	58	35.6	48	34.8	0.8
Percentages greater for private institutions					
Common sophomore-year experience	21	12.9	32	23.2	10.9
Writing skills	16	9.8	23	16.7	6.9
Oral communication skills	17	10.4	22	15.9	5.5
Career exploration and/or preparation	77	47.2	72	52.2	5.0
Intercultural competence, diversity skills, or engaging with different perspectives	24	14.7	27	19.6	4.9
Analytical, critical-thinking, or problem-solving skills	23	14.1	26	18.8	4.7
Integrative and applied learning	15	9.2	17	12.3	3.1
Student–faculty interaction	42	25.8	39	28.3	2.5
Developmental education, remediation, and/or review	5	3.1	7	5.1	2.0
Health and wellness	24	14.7	23	16.7	2.0
Major exploration	44	27.0	40	29.0	2.0
Discipline-specific knowledge	21	12.9	20	14.5	1.6
Digital literacy	9	5.5	9	6.5	1.0
Project planning, teamwork, or management skills	12	7.4	11	8.0	0.6
Personal exploration or development	36	22.1	31	22.5	0.4
Connection with the institution or campus	48	29.4	41	29.7	0.3
Introduction to the liberal arts	9	5.5	8	5.8	0.3
Total	163	100.0	138	100.0	0.0

Length of Time Institutions Have Focused on the Sophomore Year

Respondents who reported that their institution included any institutional activity with a specific focus on the sophomore year were asked to indicate how long their campus had been engaged in those efforts. Nearly 70% of participating institutions reported that their institutional activities have been around for five years or less. Alternately, more than 30% of the institutions have had some efforts focused on sophomores for six years or more, with 15.4% having institutional activities more than a decade old and 5.0% having programs with more than 20 years in existence. Additionally, despite evidence that community colleges were among institutions with the least coordinated initiatives, on average, sophomore-year programs have been in place longer at community colleges – 29% reported that they have engaged in this work for more than 10 years, compared to 12.9% of four-year institutions. The time since initiation of a sophomore-year focus did not differ for public and private institutions.

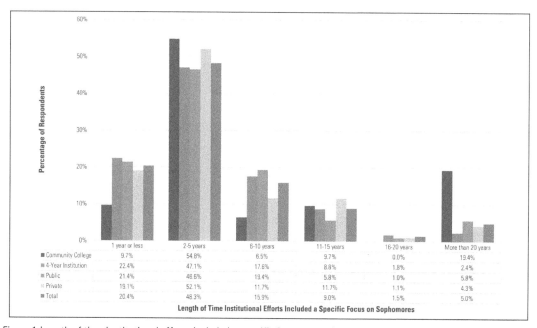

	1 year or less	2-5 years	6-10 years	11-15 years	16-20 years	More than 20 years
■ Community College	9.7%	54.8%	6.5%	9.7%	0.0%	19.4%
■ 4-Year Institution	22.4%	47.1%	17.6%	8.8%	1.8%	2.4%
■ Public	21.4%	46.6%	19.4%	5.8%	1.0%	5.8%
■ Private	19.1%	52.1%	11.7%	11.7%	1.1%	4.3%
■ Total	20.4%	48.3%	15.9%	9.0%	1.5%	5.0%

Length of Time Institutional Efforts Included a Specific Focus on Sophomores

Figure 1. Length of time institutional efforts included a specific focus on sophomores.

Characteristics of Sophomore-Year Initiatives

More than half of all participating institutions (51.1%) reported offering at least one initiative specifically or intentionally geared toward sophomore students. This finding follows a trend of increased adoption of sophomore-year initiatives on campuses as found in previous administrations of the NSSYI (2005: 33.5%; 2008: 36.5%; 2014: 46.1%; Young et al., 2015). Notably, this finding may depend on who responded to the survey: Institutions with sophomore-specific programs on campuses may be likely to respond to a survey cataloging such initiatives, thus inflating the estimate of the prevalence of these activities on campuses.

In the 2019 NSSYI, four-year institutions were more likely (54.5%) than community colleges (34.0%) to offer initiatives specifically geared toward sophomores. Additionally, private institutions were more likely than public schools to offer these (54.3% vs. 48.8%, respectively). Despite the prevalence of reported efforts associated with sophomore student success, nearly 5% of all participants indicated that they did not know if their institution offered sophomore-year initiatives. Additional details about initiatives reported are detailed in the sections that follow.

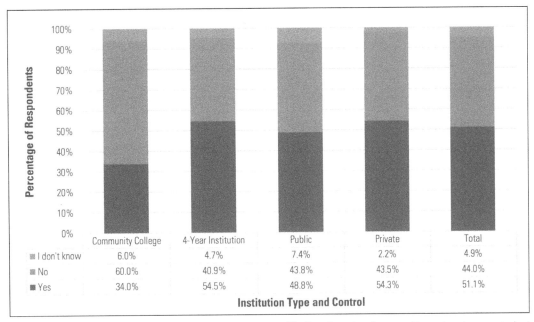

Figure 2. Institutional responses to the existence of initiatives specifically or intentionally geared toward sophomore students.

Initiatives Utilized to Meet Sophomore Objectives

To better understand how institutions position sophomore programs to meet the goals they have outlined for their students, we examined the efforts reported by institutional personnel. Participants were asked to select all initiatives (e.g., programs, activities, courses) offered by their institutions from a list of 29 (see Tables 4 and 5). The 2019 NSSYI included items to identify the initiatives associated with institutional objectives for the sophomore year and to identify the initiatives that served the highest proportion of students. Career exploration was the most popular initiative across all institutions (60.3%), followed closely by academic advising (58.3%). Other frequently reported sophomore-year initiatives included career planning (52.6%), academic coaching or mentoring (39.1%), leadership development (34.6%), major exploration and selection (34.6%), campus-based events (e.g., common reading experiences, dinners, fairs, and more; 32.7%), and early-alert systems (30.8%).

The most prevalent sophomore-year initiative offered at community colleges was academic advising (76.5%), followed by career planning (70.6%; see Table 4). Four-year institutions most frequently offered career exploration (61.9%) and academic advising (56.1%). These findings are consistent with the 2014 administration of the NSSYI, which found advising and career exploration to be the most frequently reported efforts (Young et al., 2015). Additionally, these efforts are likely to be especially useful for promoting student success, as research has found that sophomores often experience difficulty with selecting an academic major and considering and planning for a career (Gordon, 1998; Graunke & Woosley, 2005).

Table 4

Initiatives Specifically or Intentionally Geared Toward Sophomores by Institutional Type

| | Institutional type | | | | |
| | Community college | | Four-year | | Difference |
Institutional initiative	Freq.	%	Freq.	%	(%)
Percentages greater for community colleges					
Academic advising	13	76.5	78	56.1	20.4
Career planning	12	70.6	70	50.4	20.2
Internships or co-ops	6	35.3	26	18.7	16.6
Financial aid	5	29.4	18	12.9	16.5
Early-alert systems	7	41.2	41	29.5	11.7
Academic coaching or mentoring	8	47.1	53	38.1	9.0
Cultural enrichment activities	3	17.6	15	10.8	6.8
Faculty or staff mentors	4	23.5	31	22.3	1.2
Leadership development	6	35.3	48	34.5	0.8
Practica or other supervised practice experiences	1	5.9	8	5.8	0.1
Percentages greater for four-year institutions					
Major exploration and selection	2	11.8	52	37.4	25.6
Residence life—sophomore live-on-campus requirement	0	0.0	33	23.7	23.7
Back-to-school events	1	5.9	41	29.5	23.6
Campus-based event (e.g., common reading experiences, dinners, fairs)	2	11.8	49	35.3	23.5
Communication or publications (e.g., social media, newsletter, emails, brochures)	2	11.8	39	28.1	16.3
Career exploration	8	47.1	86	61.9	14.8
Residence life—sophomore-specific living learning community	0	0.0	20	14.4	14.4
Credit-bearing course (e.g., sophomore seminar)	0	0.0	19	13.7	13.7
Residence life—sophomore-specific residential curriculum	0	0.0	18	12.9	12.9
Student government	1	5.9	26	18.7	12.8
Peer mentoring by sophomores	3	17.6	39	28.1	10.5
Undergraduate research	2	11.8	29	20.9	9.1
Service learning or community service	3	17.6	37	26.6	9.0
Off-campus event (e.g., retreat, outdoor adventure)	1	5.9	19	13.7	7.8
Study abroad	2	11.8	27	19.4	7.6
Peer mentors for sophomores	2	11.8	26	18.7	6.9
Opportunities to co-teach	0	0.0	9	6.5	6.5
Course-specific support for classes with high D/F/W rates	2	11.8	25	18.0	6.2
Other	2	11.8	19	13.7	1.9
Learning communities	2	11.8	18	12.9	1.1
Total	17	100.0	139	100.0	0.0

Table 5

Initiatives Specifically or Intentionally Geared Toward Sophomores by Institutional Control

| | Institutional control | | | | Difference |
| | Public | | Private | | |
Institutional initiative	Freq.	%	Freq.	%	(%)
Percentages greater for public institutions					
Course-specific support for classes with high D/F/W rates	18	22.8	9	12.2	10.6
Off-campus event (e.g., retreat, outdoor adventure)	13	16.5	7	9.5	7.0
Academic advising	48	60.8	40	54.1	6.7
Peer mentors for sophomores	17	21.5	11	14.9	6.6
Financial aid	13	16.5	8	10.8	5.7
Academic coaching or mentoring	32	40.5	26	35.1	5.4
Residence life—sophomore-specific residential curriculum	11	13.9	7	9.5	4.4
Other	12	15.2	9	12.2	3.0
Internships or co-ops	17	21.5	14	18.9	2.6
Career exploration	49	62.0	44	59.5	2.5
Communication or publications (e.g., social media, newsletter, emails, brochures)	21	26.6	18	24.3	2.3
Opportunities to co-teach	5	6.3	4	5.4	0.9
Percentages greater for private institutions					
Residence life—sophomore live-on-campus requirement	7	8.9	26	35.1	26.2
Campus-based event (e.g., common reading experiences, dinners, fairs)	20	25.3	30	40.5	15.2
Student government	9	11.4	17	23.0	11.6
Leadership development	23	29.1	30	40.5	11.4
Back-to-school events	18	22.8	23	31.1	8.3
Service learning or community service	17	21.5	22	29.7	8.2
Study abroad	12	15.2	17	23.0	7.8
Major exploration and selection	25	31.6	29	39.2	7.6
Early-alert systems	22	27.8	25	33.8	6.0
Peer mentoring by sophomores	19	24.1	22	29.7	5.6
Learning communities	8	10.1	11	14.9	4.8
Practica or other supervised practice experiences	3	3.8	6	8.1	4.3
Residence life—sophomore-specific living learning community	9	11.4	11	14.9	3.5
Credit-bearing course (e.g., sophomore seminar)	9	11.4	10	13.5	2.1
Cultural enrichment activities	8	10.1	9	12.2	2.1
Faculty or staff mentors	17	21.5	17	23.0	1.5
Career planning	41	51.9	39	52.7	0.8
Percentages equal across institution control					
Undergraduate research	16	20.3	15	20.3	0.0
Total	79	100.0	74	100.0	0.0

Community colleges had different patterns of initiatives than four-year institutions (see Table 4). At community colleges, the most common initiatives included academic coaching or mentoring (47.1%), career exploration (47.1%), and early-alert systems (41.2%). Community colleges were more likely than four-year schools to offer the following initiatives: academic advising (76.5% vs. 56.1%), career planning (70.6% vs. 50.4%), early-alert systems (41.2% vs. 29.5%), financial aid (29.4% vs. 12.9%), and internships or co-ops (35.3% vs. 18.7%). Four-year institutions most frequently offered career exploration (61.9%) and academic advising (56.1%). Other common sophomore-year initiatives included career planning (50.4%), academic coaching or mentoring (38.1%), and major exploration and selection (37.4%). Four-year schools were more likely to offer the following initiatives with a focus on sophomore-year students than community colleges: back-to-school events (including any large-scale gathering at the beginning of the school year that targets sophomores en masse at a one-time event; 29.5% vs. 5.9%), campus-based events (35.3% vs. 11.8%), career exploration (61.9% vs. 47.1%), communication or publications (e.g., social media, newsletters, emails, or brochures; 28.1% vs. 11.8%), credit-bearing courses (e.g., a sophomore-year seminar; 13.7% vs. 0.0%), major exploration and selection (37.4% vs. 11.8%), peer mentors for sophomores (18.7% vs. 11.8%), student government (18.7% vs. 5.9%), and undergraduate research opportunities (20.9% vs. 11.8%).

Variations in initiatives between public and private schools were also discovered (see Table 5). Public institutions in the sample were more likely to offer the following initiatives than private schools: academic advising (60.8% vs. 54.1%), course-specific support for classes with high D/F/W rates (22.8% vs. 12.2%), off-campus events (e.g., retreat, outdoor adventure; 16.5% vs. 9.5%), peer mentors for sophomores (21.5% vs. 14.9%), and sophomore-specific residential curricula (13.9% vs. 9.5%). Private institutions offered more of the following than publics: campus-based events (e.g., common reading experiences, dinners, or fairs; 40.5% vs. 25.3%), leadership development (40.5% vs. 29.1%), practica or other supervised practice experiences (8.1% vs. 3.8%), and student government (23.0% vs. 11.4%).

Crucial Programs Designated to Reach Objectives Associated with Sophomore-Year Experience

To determine which efforts institutions found most crucial to sophomore student success, we asked participants to identify the primary, or most important, sophomore-year initiatives by which campuswide objectives were met. Participants could select up to five initiatives that their campus believes to be the most important for sophomores (see Tables 6 and 7). Academic advising was reported as the most important initiative associated with the sophomore year at community colleges (81.3%), four-year schools (58.4%), and across the overall sample (60.8%). Other frequently named initiatives, many of which are advising-related, included career exploration (37.9%), career planning (22.9%), major exploration and selection (22.2%), academic coaching or mentoring (19.0%), and leadership development (19.0%). While academic advising remained the most frequently identified, the gap between it and the other programs was not nearly as pronounced when institutions were given the chance to identify the other initiatives used to meet sophomore-year objectives.

Disaggregating these results by institutional type (see Table 6), we found that a substantially larger percentage of community colleges reported the use of academic advising to meet sophomore-year objectives (81.3%) than did their four-year counterparts (58.4%). Community colleges also frequently named academic coaching or mentoring (25.0%), career planning (25.0%), early-alert systems (25.0%), and leadership development (18.8%) as the primary means by which they achieve their sophomore-year objectives. Similarly, four-year campuses reported career exploration (40.9%), major exploration and selection (24.1%), career planning (22.6%), and leadership development (19.0%) as crucial sophomore programs used to meet their objectives.

Comparisons based on institutional control (see Table 7) show that 66.7% of public institutions reported using academic advising as a primary vehicle for meeting goals for sophomore students on their campuses, whereas only 54.2% of private institutions did so. In addition, public colleges and universities listed career exploration (32.1%), academic coaching or mentoring (24.4%), career planning (21.8%), and early-alert systems (19.2%) as initiatives frequently used to achieve sophomore-year objectives. Participants from private institutions also reported that career exploration (44.4%), major exploration and selection (30.6%), career planning (23.6%), and second-year live-on-campus requirements (22.2%) were primary ways in which they met campuswide objectives.

Table 6

Primary Sophomore-Year Programs by Which Campuswide Objectives for Sophomores Are Met by Institutional Type

| | Institutional type | | | | Difference |
| | Community college | | Four-year | | |
Institutional initiative	Freq.	%	Freq.	%	(%)
Percentages greater for community colleges					
Academic advising	13	81.3	80	58.4	22.9
Practica or other supervised practice experiences	2	12.5	0	0.0	12.5
Early-alert systems	4	25.0	19	13.9	11.1
Cultural enrichment activities	2	12.5	2	1.5	11.0
Undergraduate research	2	12.5	7	5.1	7.4
Academic coaching or mentoring	4	25.0	25	18.2	6.8
Financial aid	2	12.5	9	6.6	5.9
Internships or co-ops	1	6.3	5	3.6	2.7
Career planning	4	25.0	31	22.6	2.4
Service learning or community service	2	12.5	15	10.9	1.6
Other	2	12.5	17	12.4	0.1
Percentages greater for four-year institutions					
Career exploration	2	12.5	56	40.9	28.4
Major exploration and selection	1	6.3	33	24.1	17.8
Residence life—sophomore live-on-campus requirement	0	0.0	20	14.6	14.6
Credit-bearing course (e.g., sophomore seminar)	0	0.0	19	13.9	13.9
Campus-based event (e.g., common reading experiences, dinners, fairs)	1	6.3	24	17.5	11.2
Back-to-school events	0	0.0	14	10.2	10.2
Study abroad	0	0.0	12	8.8	8.8
Residence life—sophomore-specific living learning community	0	0.0	11	8.0	8.0
Residence life—sophomore-specific residential curriculum	0	0.0	11	8.0	8.0
Communication or publications (e.g., social media, newsletter, emails, brochures)	1	6.3	19	13.9	7.6
Peer mentoring by sophomores	1	6.3	17	12.4	6.1
Course-specific support for classes with high D/F/W rates	0	0.0	8	5.8	5.8
Off-campus event (e.g., retreat, outdoor adventure)	0	0.0	7	5.1	5.1
Faculty or staff mentors	1	6.3	14	10.2	3.9
Learning communities	0	0.0	4	2.9	2.9
Opportunities to co-teach	0	0.0	3	2.2	2.2
Student government	0	0.0	3	2.2	2.2
Peer mentors for sophomores	1	6.3	8	5.8	0.5
Leadership development	3	18.8	26	19.0	0.2
Total	16	100.0	137	100.0	0.0

Table 7

Primary Sophomore-Year Programs by Which Campuswide Objectives for Sophomores Are Met by Institutional Control

| Institutional initiative | Institutional control | | | | Difference (%) |
| | Public | | Private | | |
	Freq.	%	Freq.	%	
Percentages greater for public institutions					
Academic advising	52	66.7	39	54.2	12.5
Academic coaching or mentoring	19	24.4	9	12.5	11.9
Other	13	16.7	6	8.3	8.4
Early-alert systems	15	19.2	8	11.1	8.1
Communication or publications (e.g., social media, newsletter, emails, brochures)	13	16.7	7	9.7	7.0
Undergraduate research	7	9.0	2	2.8	6.2
Financial aid	7	9.0	3	4.2	4.8
Cultural enrichment activities	3	3.8	0	0.0	3.8
Course-specific support for classes with high D/F/W rates	5	6.4	2	2.8	3.6
Peer mentors for sophomores	6	7.7	3	4.2	3.5
Residence life—sophomore-specific residential curriculum	7	9.0	4	5.6	3.4
Practica or other supervised practice experiences	2	2.6	0	0.0	2.6
Faculty or staff mentors	8	10.3	7	9.7	0.6
Percentages greater for private institutions					
Residence life—sophomore live-on-campus requirement	4	5.1	16	22.2	17.1
Major exploration and selection	12	15.4	22	30.6	15.2
Career exploration	25	32.1	32	44.4	12.3
Study abroad	2	2.6	10	13.9	11.3
Peer mentoring by sophomores	7	9.0	11	15.3	6.3
Back-to-school events	6	7.7	8	11.1	3.4
Leadership development	14	17.9	15	20.8	2.9
Student government	0	0.0	2	2.8	2.8
Service learning or community service	8	10.3	9	12.5	2.2
Residence life—sophomore-specific living learning community	5	6.4	6	8.3	1.9
Career planning	17	21.8	17	23.6	1.8
Off-campus event (e.g., retreat, outdoor adventure)	3	3.8	4	5.6	1.8
Opportunities to co-teach	1	1.3	2	2.8	1.5
Credit-bearing course (e.g., sophomore seminar)	9	11.5	9	12.5	1.0
Internships or co-ops	3	3.8	3	4.2	0.4
Learning communities	2	2.6	2	2.8	0.2
Percentages equal across institutions					
Campus-based event (e.g., common reading experiences, dinners, fairs)	13	16.7	12	16.7	0.0
Total	78	100.0	72	100.0	0.0

Initiatives Reaching the Highest Proportion of Sophomores

Respondents were asked to select the sophomore-year initiative on campus that reached the highest proportion of sophomore students (i.e., predominant initiative; see Tables 8 and 9). Similar to the findings from the 2014 administration of the NSSYI (Young et al., 2015), academic advising was the service identified by the greatest percentage of institutions (40.0%) by a wide margin. Academic advising was reported six times more than the two initiatives tied for second place, sophomore live-on-campus requirement (6.5%) and career exploration (6.5%). These results nearly replicate those from the 2014 administration, with the exception of career exploration, which was present at a greater percentage of campuses and which moved from eighth on the list to second in prevalence among respondents

When the predominant sophomore initiative is disaggregated by institutional type (see Table 8), results show that academic advising is the most prevalent program at both four-year and community colleges. However, a comparatively greater proportion of community colleges reported academic advising as the predominant sophomore-year initiative (52.9%) than did four-year colleges and universities (38.4%). Academic coaching or mentoring (11.8%) and career planning (11.8%) were tied for the second most frequently named programs by community colleges. In contrast, four-year institutions identified sophomore year on-campus living requirements (7.2%) and career exploration (6.5%) as the predominant initiatives following academic advising.

Comparisons based on institutional control also revealed patterns of interest (see Table 9). Academic advising was the most frequently named initiative among both public and private institutions, although the prevalence was slightly higher at public institutions (43.0%) than at private institutions (35.6%). Academic coaching or mentoring (8.9%), sophomore-year communications or publications (6.3%), and early-alert systems (6.3%) followed in frequency among public institutions. Private institutions also named sophomore live-on-campus requirements (11.0%) and career exploration (9.6%) as the predominant initiatives focused on sophomores on their campuses.

These results point to a few important implications. First, the evidence suggests that institutions are using a multifaceted approach to support sophomores, particularly as it relates to academic support, major exploration and selection, and career development. Moreover, there are important sophomore-year initiatives that may not reach large proportions of students on campuses but could be related to institutional markers of student success. Some examples may include specialized programs for minoritized students, such as TRIO-based programs that serve as sophomore-year follow-ups to Upward Bound or GEAR UP. Thus, we encourage campuses to consider the purpose and function of sophomore-year initiatives and not discount programs that may not necessarily reach the greatest number of students but may be impactful to specific student populations. Creating a comprehensive, coordinated, and integrated approach is critical in maximizing the effectiveness of a campuswide success agenda.

Table 8

Initiatives Reaching the Highest Proportion of Sophomores by Institutional Type

| | Institutional type | | | | Difference |
| | Community college | | Four-year | | |
Institutional initiative	Freq.	%	Freq.	%	(%)
Percentages greater for community colleges					
Academic advising	9	52.9	53	38.4	14.5
Career planning	2	11.8	3	2.2	9.6
Academic coaching or mentoring	2	11.8	7	5.1	6.7
Peer mentors for sophomores	1	5.9	1	0.7	5.2
Leadership development	1	5.9	4	2.9	3.0
Other	1	5.9	5	3.6	2.3
Percentages greater for four-year institutions					
Residence life—sophomore live-on-campus requirement	0	0.0	10	7.2	7.2
Campus-based event (e.g., common reading experiences, dinners, fairs)	0	0.0	6	4.3	4.3
Communication or publications (e.g., social media, newsletter, emails, brochures)	0	0.0	6	4.3	4.3
Early-alert systems	0	0.0	6	4.3	4.3
Back-to-school events	0	0.0	5	3.6	3.6
Credit-bearing course (e.g., sophomore seminar)	0	0.0	5	3.6	3.6
Major exploration and selection	0	0.0	3	2.2	2.2
Residence life—sophomore-specific residential curriculum	0	0.0	3	2.2	2.2
Service learning or community service	0	0.0	2	1.4	1.4
Study abroad	0	0.0	2	1.4	1.4
Faculty or staff mentors	0	0.0	1	0.7	0.7
Financial aid	0	0.0	1	0.7	0.7
Internships or co-ops	0	0.0	1	0.7	0.7
Learning communities	0	0.0	1	0.7	0.7
Off-campus event (e.g., retreat, outdoor adventure)	0	0.0	1	0.7	0.7
Peer mentoring by sophomores	0	0.0	1	0.7	0.7
Residence life—sophomore-specific living learning community	0	0.0	1	0.7	0.7
Student government	0	0.0	1	0.7	0.7
Career exploration	1	5.9	9	6.5	0.6
Percentages equal across institution type					
Course-specific support for classes with high D/F/W rates	0	0.0	0	0.0	0.0
Cultural enrichment activities	0	0.0	0	0.0	0.0
Opportunities to co-teach	0	0.0	0	0.0	0.0
Practica or other supervised practice experiences	0	0.0	0	0.0	0.0
Undergraduate research	0	0.0	0	0.0	0.0
Total	17	100.0	138	100.0	0.0

Table 9

Initiatives Reaching the Highest Proportion of Sophomores by Institutional Control

| | Institutional control | | | | Difference |
| | Public | | Private | | |
Institutional initiative	Freq.	%	Freq.	%	(%)
Percentages greater for public institutions					
Academic advising	34	43.0	26	35.6	7.4
Academic coaching or mentoring	7	8.9	2	2.7	6.2
Communication or publications (e.g., social media, newsletter, emails, brochures)	5	6.3	1	1.4	4.9
Early-alert systems	5	6.3	1	1.4	4.9
Career planning	3	3.8	1	1.4	2.4
Other	4	5.1	2	2.7	2.4
Financial aid	1	1.3	0	0.0	1.3
Learning communities	1	1.3	0	0.0	1.3
Off-campus event (e.g., retreat, outdoor adventure)	1	1.3	0	0.0	1.3
Peer mentoring by sophomores	1	1.3	0	0.0	1.3
Residence life—sophomore-specific residential curriculum	2	2.5	1	1.4	1.1
Percentages greater for private institutions					
Residence life—sophomore live-on-campus requirement	2	2.5	8	11.0	8.5
Career exploration	3	3.8	7	9.6	5.8
Back-to-school events	1	1.3	4	5.5	4.2
Campus-based event (e.g., common reading experiences, dinners, fairs)	2	2.5	4	5.5	3.0
Study abroad	0	0.0	2	2.7	2.7
Credit-bearing course (e.g., sophomore seminar)	2	2.5	3	4.1	1.6
Leadership development	2	2.5	3	4.1	1.6
Faculty or staff mentors	0	0.0	1	1.4	1.4
Internships or co-ops	0	0.0	1	1.4	1.4
Major exploration and selection	1	1.3	2	2.7	1.4
Residence life—sophomore-specific living learning community	0	0.0	1	1.4	1.4
Student government	0	0.0	1	1.4	1.4
Peer mentors for sophomores	1	1.3	1	1.4	0.1
Service learning or community service	1	1.3	1	1.4	0.1
Percentages equal across institutions					
Course-specific support for classes with high D/F/W rates	0	0.0	0	0.0	0.0
Cultural enrichment activities	0	0.0	0	0.0	0.0
Opportunities to co-teach	0	0.0	0	0.0	0.0
Practica or other supervised practice experiences	0	0.0	0	0.0	0.0
Undergraduate research	0	0.0	0	0.0	0.0
Total	79	100.0	73	100.0	0.0

Academic Advising and the Sophomore Year

We underscore that academic advising was both the most frequently reported and one of the most crucial activities that institutions had in place for sophomores in both the 2019 and 2014 administrations of NSSYI (cf. Young et al., 2015). These findings confirm prior research that highlights academic advising as a significant, common, and integral initiative associated with sophomore student success (Schreiner, 2018). As Young et al. (2015) noted, "it would be rare to find an institution where each student was not assigned an academic advisor" (p. 16). It is important to note that while advising does reach a large proportion of students (as most students interact with an advisor at some point during their undergraduate career), information about the frequency and quality of these interactions is understudied. Moreover, qualitative research on the nature and activities on sophomore-specific advising would provide greater insight into interactions within advising meetings.

Results from the 2019 NYSSI revealed that advising reaches the highest proportion of sophomores, with 40% of institutions indicating such (see Figure 3). Advising is more prevalent at community colleges (52.9%) than four-year schools (38.4%) and was reported to be the primary sophomore-year program by which the campuswide objectives for sophomores are met (at 60.8% of all institutions). Within the sample, 70.0% of institutions reported that academic advising reaches 91% to 100% of their sophomore students. Furthermore, advising is required of sophomore students at 66.0% of institutions (56.3% of community colleges and 67.2% of four-year schools). At 25.0% of community colleges, no sophomore students are required to participate in academic advising; this is the case for 13.4% of four-year institutions. Respondents most frequently indicated that students who were required to participate in academic advising included those on probationary status (82.8% of the institutions), student athletes (65.5%), and undeclared students (51.7%). It is important to note that the 2019 NSSYI did not ask institutions (a) what mechanisms are in place to require students to meet with advisors (e.g., by placing a registration hold or meeting with advisors to receive a registration code) or (b) how frequently students are required to interact with an academic advisor and what the student-advisor interaction looks like in these meetings.

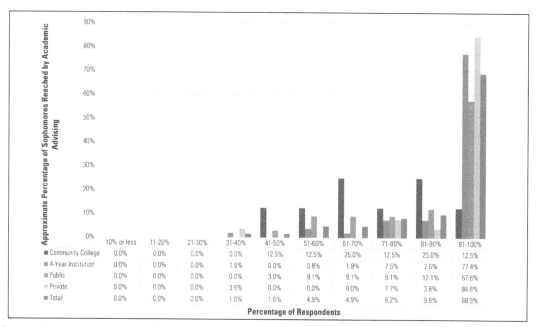

Figure 3. Approximate percentage of sophomores reached by academic advising.

The vast majority of institutions target all enrolled sophomore students through academic advising (86.9% of the overall sample: 75.0% of community colleges; 88.7% of four-year schools; 75.8% of publics; and 100.0%

of privates). Participants indicated that their institutions focus on specific populations of sophomore students through advising, including students on probationary status (36.1%), student athletes (31.1%), and academically underprepared students (24.6%). We note that while institutions were able to identify which groups of students advising may be targeted toward, respondents were unable to explain their focus on particular student populations. At most institutions, academic advising for sophomores has been in place for less than 20 years (see Figure 4). Within community colleges in the sample, the majority of advising has been in place for the last decade, with 37.5% reporting advising has been in place for 3 to 5 years and an additional 25.0% reporting that it has been in place for 6 to 10 years. At four-year institutions, almost half the sample (49.0%) indicated that advising has been in place for sophomores during the last 15 years.

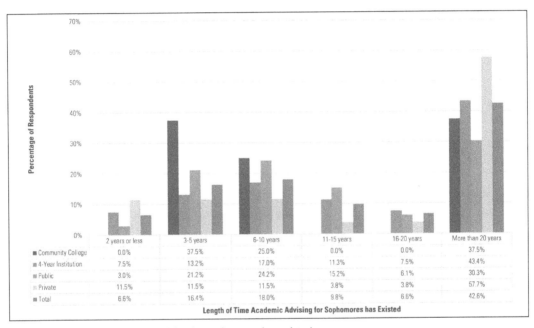

	2 years or less	3-5 years	6-10 years	11-15 years	16-20 years	More than 20 years
■ Community College	0.0%	37.5%	25.0%	0.0%	0.0%	37.5%
■ 4-Year Institution	7.5%	13.2%	17.0%	11.3%	7.5%	43.4%
■ Public	3.0%	21.2%	24.2%	15.2%	6.1%	30.3%
▨ Private	11.5%	11.5%	11.5%	3.8%	3.8%	57.7%
■ Total	6.6%	16.4%	18.0%	9.8%	6.6%	42.6%

Length of Time Academic Advising for Sophomores has Existed

Figure 4. Length of time academic advising for sophomores has existed.

Academic advising can be a valuable tool for fostering engagement among sophomore students (Young et al., 2015), particularly in connecting students to faculty (Schreiner & Tobolowsky, 2018) and instilling a sense of purpose and community on campus (Gahagan, 2018). However, advising has been identified as one of the areas in which sophomores are least satisfied (Young et al., 2015). As Schreiner and Tobolowsky (2018) noted, "dissatisfaction with advising in the sophomore year arises from two specific deficits: a lack of connection to career planning and a lack of in-depth personalized attention" (p. 62). Sophomores frequently need conversations with interested student-services staff, advisors, and faculty as well as mentoring that will provide the deep ongoing relationships that second-year students are looking for (Schreiner & Tobolowsky, 2018). This finding has implications for sophomore student success generally as well as for specific groups of students.

Issues associated with advising, such as helping students develop major certainty, providing opportunities for student–faculty interaction, and developing a sense of community on campus are among pathways to sophomore student thriving (Schreiner, 2018; Young et al., 2015). However, students' experiences may differ by racial and ethnic groups and across institutional types (e.g., at predominately White institutions or minority-serving institutions). For example, among participants in the Sophomore Experiences Survey, Black students interacted with faculty more than students from other racial groups, yet they benefitted the least from that interaction (Lundberg & Schreiner, 2004; Schreiner, 2018). Notwithstanding, when the interaction was positive or rewarding for Black sophomores, it contributed more to their thriving than it did for any other racial or ethnic group (Schreiner, 2018). Similarly, Asian American and Latinx students interact infrequently with faculty and experience little benefit (Kim, 2010). Yet student–faculty interactions are beneficial for Asian American students when the conversations are connected directly to their major and for Latinx sophomores when the exchange centers on personal development and when faculty express a personal interest in them (Schreiner, 2018; Young et al., 2015). Training and professional development for advisors that is culturally responsive and that focuses on building upon students' strengths and knowledge can be one way for advisors to establish meaningful connections with students (Gay, 2010).

On the 2019 NSSYI, participants were asked to rate to what extent certain high-impact characteristics were present in academic advising for sophomores using a scale of 1 (indicating the element is not present) to 5 (meaning the element is pervasive throughout the initiative). One of these elements included "interactions with faculty and peers about substantive matters." A sizable number (42.4%) of participating institutions indicated that this element was partially present in their advising initiatives. An additional 20.3% of schools responded this prompt with a 4, and 18.6% responded with a 5. Thus, taken together with the low rates of satisfaction overall and reported differences in these experiences among sophomores from racially and ethnically minoritized groups, it is important for those engaged in advising sophomores to keep in mind that although student–faculty interaction is important, the quality rather than the frequency of the interaction is predictive of successful outcomes (Kim & Sax, 2017).

The 2019 NSSYI also uncovered significant objectives related to academic advising. The three most important objectives across the overall sample included academic planning (88.5%), career exploration and/or preparation (32.8%), and major exploration (29.5%). At community colleges, objectives cited as most significant were academic planning (87.5%); career exploration and/or preparation (37.5%); analytical, critical-thinking, or problem-solving skills (25.0%); and major exploration (25.0%). At four-year institutions, academic planning was the most frequently reported objective (88.7%), followed by academic success strategies (34.0%) and career exploration and/or preparation (32.1%).

Reporting on assessment and evaluation practices, 51.0% of institutions said they had not formally assessed or evaluated academic advising for sophomores within the past three years at the time the 2019 NYSSI was distributed. An additional 20% of participants did not know if academic advising for sophomores had been assessed or evaluated. Of the institutions that had participated in assessment, 78.6% conducted an analysis of institutional data (e.g., grade point average, retention rates, graduation rates). Half reported using a locally designed survey instrument, and 35.7% conducted direct assessment of student learning outcomes. Less frequently used methods included individual interviews with faculty (14.3%), students (11.9%), and orientation staff (14.3%). The most frequently assessed outcomes included academic success strategies (66.7%); career exploration and/or preparation (60.0%); and persistence, retention, or third-year return rates (60.0%). Among the least frequently assessed outcomes were graduate or professional school preparation (6.7%) and social support networks (e.g., friendships; 6.7%). Additionally, 75.0% of schools participated in ongoing professional development and training for advisors, and over half (51.4%) participated in campuswide assessment and planning.

Sophomore-Year Initiatives as High-Impact Practices

The 2014 administration of the NSSYI introduced the inquiry into the extent to which primary sophomore-year initiatives met the elements of high-impact practices (HIPs) as identified by Kuh (2013). Although many of the sophomore-year programs that were identified by participants were not in the original list of 10 HIPs identified by the Association of American Colleges and Universities (Kuh, 2008), it stands to reason that if certain sophomore-year programs are put in place to improve student outcomes, the elements of high-quality educational environments would serve as a framework by which we can evaluate the potential effectiveness of these initiatives.

In a report that described scaling HIPs and how institutions might identify and create new ones, Kuh (2013) identified eight key elements of high-impact practice: (a) performance expectations set at appropriately high levels; (b) significant investment of time and effort by students over an extended period of time;

(c) interactions with faculty and peers about substantive matters; (d) experiences with diversity, wherein students are exposed to and must contend with people and circumstances that differ from those with which students are familiar; (e) frequent, timely, and constructive feedback; (f) periodic, structured opportunities to reflect and integrate learning; (g) opportunities to discover relevance of learning through real-world applications; and (h) public demonstration of competence. These eight elements represent a set of standards for excellence in student-success initiatives and represent the foundational principles that give HIPs their impact.

In the 2019 NSSYI, we used Kuh's (2013) framework to investigate the educational effectiveness of sophomore-year initiatives. Participants were asked to identify the extent to which each of the eight elements of high-impact practice was present in the predominant sophomore-year initiative. The respondents from participating institutions were asked to rate the presence of each element on a 5-point scale that ranged from 1 (element is not present) to 5 (element is pervasive throughout). Seven in eight elements were reported by 50% or more of the participants as at least partially present in their predominant sophomore-year initiatives (see Figure 5). The element most frequently identified by institutional respondents was interactions with faculty and peers around substantive matters; 80% of respondents reported that element was at least partially present in their sophomore-year initiative. Five of the elements were named by approximately two thirds of participants, including high performance expectations, investment of time and effort, frequent and timely feedback, opportunities to reflect and integrate learning, and learning through real-world applications. The only element that was named as partially present by less than half of respondents was public demonstration of competence.

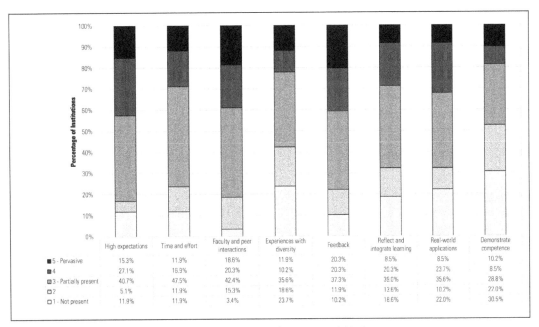

Figure 5. Elements of high-impact practices evident among sophomore-year initiatives.

Due to the overwhelming prevalence of academic advising as a primary initiative, the other sophomore-year initiatives reported in the 2019 NSSYI were grouped according to the categories developed by Young et al. (2015; see Table 10). Using this scheme, the four sophomore-year initiatives most predominant were academic advising, career- and major-focused initiatives, residential initiatives, and academic support. Within academic advising, the elements most frequently reported included appropriately high performance expectations (83.1%) and interactions with faculty and peers around substantive matters (81.4%). The elements most frequently reported within career- and major-related initiatives included opportunities to reflect and integrate learning (94.1%) and learning through real-world applications (88.2%). Within residential initiatives, experiences with diversity was the most frequently named element of HIPs present (85.7%). Interactions with faculty and peers was the next most prevalent element within residential second-year initiatives (64.3%). Finally, participants from institutions with academic support as a predominant sophomore program most frequently reported learning through real-world applications (91.7%); interactions with faculty and peers (83.3%); and frequent, timely, and constructive feedback (83.3.%) as elements of HIPs present.

Table 10

Percentage of Institutions Reporting Presence of Elements of High-Impact Practice by Category of Sophomore-Year Initiative

Element of high-impact practice	Academic advising (%)	Career- and major-related (%)	Residential initiatives (%)	Academic support (%)
Appropriately high performance expectations	83.1			
Investment of time and effort				
Interactions with faculty and peers about substantive matters	81.4		64.3	83.3
Experiences with diversity			85.7	
Frequent, timely, and constructive feedback				83.3
Opportunities to reflect and integrate learning		94.1		
Real-world applications		88.2		91.7
Public demonstration of competence				

Note. The two most frequently reported elements of high-impact practices are reported for each type of sophomore-year initiatives. All other percentages have been suppressed.

Campuswide Efforts Associated with Sophomore-Year Experiences

Institutions used a variety of efforts to improve success among sophomores. Efforts can be defined as projects conducted at a campuswide or administrative level that gather data from initiatives and activities in which students participate. Furthermore, efforts are means that can be used to better understand sophomore students' experiences and the ways in which institutional structures and processes can improve initiatives for students. Frequently reported efforts across the overall sample included retention studies (33.4%), student-services programming (27.3%), and institutional assessment (23.7%).

At community colleges, institutional assessment was the most frequently reported effort (26.0%), followed by advising studies (22.0%) and employment or job-placement study (20.0%; see Table 11). Community colleges were more likely to have employment or job-placement studies for sophomores (20.0%) and pathways programs or meta-majors for sophomores (18.0%) than four-year institutions were (8.1% and 6.2%, respectively). At four-year institutions, the most prevalent efforts included retention studies (36.8%), student-services programming (29.8%), and institutional assessment (23.3%).

Pathways programs or meta-majors for sophomores (12.3%) were more likely to be offered at the public institutions in the sample than at the private schools (3.6%; see Table 12). Public schools were also more likely than private schools to have graduation studies related to sophomores (8.6% vs. 3.6%, respectively). On the other hand, staff at private institutions were more likely to engage in accreditation efforts focused on the sophomore year (e.g., an action plan or quality enhancement plan; 8.7%) and retention studies with a specific focus on sophomores (39.1%) than staff at public schools (2.5% and 28.2%, respectively).

Table 11

Efforts Focused on the Sophomore Year by Institutional Type

| | Institutional type | | | | |
| | Community college | | Four-year | | Difference |
Institutional effort	Freq.	%	Freq.	%	(%)
Percentages greater for community colleges					
Advising study	11	22.0	50	19.4	−2.6
Employment or job-placement study	10	20.0	21	8.1	−11.9
Graduation study	7	14.0	13	5.0	−9.0
Institutional assessment	13	26.0	60	23.3	−2.7
Pathways programs or meta-majors	9	18.0	16	6.2	−11.8
Program self-study	4	8.0	17	6.6	−1.4
Other, please specify	5	10.0	17	6.6	−3.4
Our institution has not engaged in any efforts with a specific focus on the sophomore year	19	38.0	87	33.7	−4.3
Percentages greater for four-year institutions					
Accreditation (e.g., Action Project or Quality Enhancement Plan focused on sophomore-year students)	1	2.0	17	6.6	4.6
Curricular or gateway course redesign	6	12.0	41	15.9	3.9
Grant-funded project	4	8.0	21	8.1	0.1
Participation in a national survey of sophomore-year students (e.g., Noel-Levitz, Sophomore Experiences Survey)	2	4.0	26	10.1	6.1
Retention study	8	16.0	95	36.8	20.8
Strategic planning	7	14.0	57	22.1	8.1
Student-services programming	7	14.0	77	29.8	15.8
Total	50	100.0	258	100.0	0.0

Table 12

Efforts Focused on the Sophomore Year by Institutional Control

| Institutional effort | Institutional control | | | | Difference |
| | Public | | Private | | |
	Freq.	%	Freq.	%	(%)
Percentages greater for public institutions					
Employment or job-placement study	16	9.8	13	9.4	-0.4
Graduation study	14	8.6	5	3.6	-5.0
Grant-funded project	14	8.6	11	8.0	-0.6
Institutional assessment	40	24.5	32	23.2	-1.3
Participation in a national survey of sophomore-year students (e.g., Noel-Levitz, Sophomore Experiences Survey)	16	9.8	12	8.7	-1.1
Pathways programs or meta-majors	20	12.3	5	3.6	-8.7
Program self-study	14	8.6	7	5.1	-3.5
Other, please specify	14	8.6	8	5.8	-2.8
Our institution has not engaged in any efforts with a specific focus on the sophomore year	59	36.2	44	31.9	-4.3
Percentages greater for private institutions					
Accreditation (e.g., Action Project or Quality Enhancement Plan focused on sophomore-year students)	4	2.5	12	8.7	6.2
Advising study	30	18.4	28	20.3	1.9
Curricular or gateway course redesign	23	14.1	23	16.7	2.6
Retention study	46	28.2	54	39.1	10.9
Strategic planning	32	19.6	31	22.5	2.9
Student-services programming	41	25.2	40	29.0	3.8
Total	163	100.0	138	100.0	0.0

While several schools in the sample reported a multitude of efforts designated to support sophomores, over a third of institutions (34.4%) indicated that they had not engaged in any efforts with a specific focus on the sophomore year, including 38.0% of community colleges and 33.7% of four-year schools. Furthermore, across the overall sample, most initiatives focused on sophomores were nascent. The majority of institutions (48.3%) expressed that their efforts had been in place for the last two to five years, including 54.8% of community colleges and 47.1% of four-year institutions. At one fifth of institutions (20.4%), student-success initiatives had included a specific focus on sophomores only within the last year or less. Additionally, most efforts at private institutions (52.1%) had focused specifically on sophomores for the last two to five years; this percentage was similar at public institutions (46.6%).

Coordination of Efforts Associated with the Sophomore-Year Experience

Participants were asked to rate how coordinated their sophomore-year initiatives were on a scale of 1 to 5, with 1 indicating efforts that were totally decentralized and 5 representing those that were centralized (see Figure 6). The most frequently reported rating across all participating institutions was the midpoint, or 3 (37.8%). This midpoint rating was prominent at community colleges (47.1%). At four-year institutions, 36.7% reported their sophomore-year initiatives were at the midpoint of this scale. Additionally, 12.2% of four-year schools reported a 1 and 24.5% reported a 2, indicating that the majority of four-year schools reported their initiatives are decentralized in some way.

When examining institutions by control, 39.2% of public institutions also selected the midpoint (3). Furthermore, 26.6% of publics selected 2, and 13.9% selected 1, indicating that the majority of public institutions described themselves as decentralized. The midpoint (3) was also the most frequently reported response option among private institutions (37.8%). However, 21.6% selected 2 on the scale, and another 21.6% selected 4. It is worth noting that the 2019 NSSYI did not ask respondents questions about why services were decentralized. As such, future research may address this gap by determining the offices in which sophomore student services are housed (e.g., student or academic affairs) and the ways in which initiatives for the sophomore year may support institutional first-year experience programs.

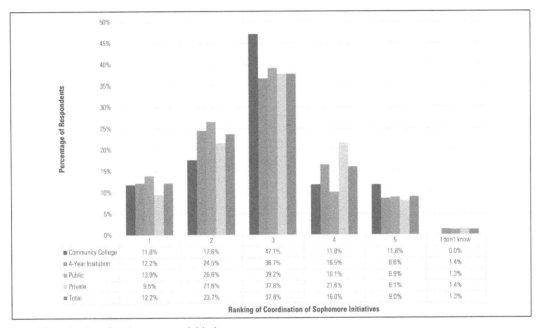

	1	2	3	4	5	I don't know
Community College	11.8%	17.6%	47.1%	11.8%	11.8%	0.0%
4-Year Insitution	12.2%	24.5%	36.7%	16.5%	8.6%	1.4%
Public	13.9%	26.6%	39.2%	10.1%	8.9%	1.3%
Private	9.5%	21.6%	37.8%	21.6%	8.1%	1.4%
Total	12.2%	23.7%	37.8%	16.0%	9.0%	1.3%

Ranking of Coordination of Sophomore Initiatives

Figure 6. Coordination of sophomore-year initiatives.

Most institutions in the overall sample (60.9%) did not have an individual staff or faculty member in charge of sophomore student programs or initiatives (see Figure 7). More community colleges (70.6%) reported that their campuses do not have a designated person for sophomore-year programs more frequently than did four-year institutions (59.7%). Public and private institutions also more frequently reported lacking an individual in charge of sophomore programs (62.0% and 60.8%, respectively). Of those institutions that did have someone responsible for sophomore programs, the majority of these individuals (73.8% of the total sample) were not dedicated to sophomore programs on a full-time basis, or approximately 40 hours per week. Approximately 74% of individuals not responsible for sophomore programs in a full-time capacity had other positions on campus, and these roles included student affairs administrators (32.4%), academic affairs administrators (29.4%), and full-time or tenure-track faculty members (20.6%).

Multiple units on campus participated in the coordination of sophomore-year initiatives (see Figure 7). Across the overall sample, these offices included academic advising (70.2%), career services (62.0%), student activities and leadership (51.2%), and academic affairs central offices (47.9%). At community colleges, academic advising (92.3%), student activities and leadership (69.2%), and career services (61.5%) were the three most participatory offices. Four-year institutions also reported frequently having their academic advising offices (67.6%) and career services offices (62.0%) participate in the coordination of sophomore-year initiatives, along with academic affairs central offices (49.1%) and student activities and leadership offices (49.1%).

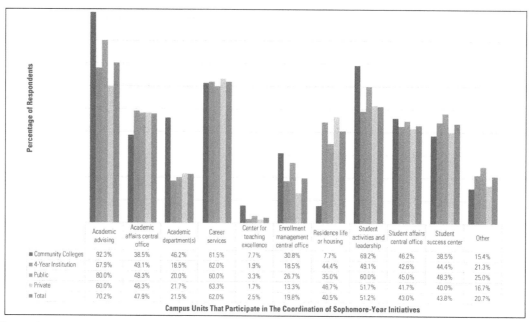

Figure 7. Campus units that participate in the coordination of sophomore-year initiatives.

Future Directions

This report revealed results from the 2019 NSSYI, including key initiatives and services associated with sophomore student success. Thinking forward, participants reported that they were considering or were in the process of developing sophomore initiatives at their institutions, including career planning (61.9%), career exploration (54.8%), and academic advising (53.6%). Community colleges most frequently reported considering or developing career planning for sophomores (91.7%), academic advising (66.7%), and early-alert systems (66.7%). The increased focus on academic advising and early-alert systems within the community college sector is not a surprise, given an increased movement toward adapting guided pathways models, which aim to embed opportunities for students to seek support from advisors throughout their academic career (American Association of Community Colleges, 2021). At four-year institutions, career planning (56.9%), career exploration (55.6%), and academic advising (51.4%) were on the horizon for participants, as well.

The 2019 NSSYI also revealed that more than one third of institutions (34.4%) indicated that they had not engaged in any efforts with a specific focus on the sophomore year. This number is lower than previous administrations of the survey: the 2014 NSSYI indicated that 46.1% of institutions offered at least one sophomore-year initiative. Research and assessment should continue to include a focus on sophomore students. The importance of the sophomore year and goals associated with student success should be communicated to all associated offices on campus and with students (Schreiner et al., 2018). Specifically, future research and practice should take note of how efforts are adopted, including the activities that are implemented, the ways that efforts are coordinated, and the ways that students interact with such services. As part of this planning, educators should continue to reflect on the following questions: How can the sophomore year, including academic advising, lead to greater levels of campus integration around student success? How might activities in the sophomore year give institutions the opportunities to support purpose, belonging, and student–faculty interaction (Schreiner et al., 2018)?

For sophomore-year initiatives to be most valuable, equity must be a crucial priority across institutions. Results from the 2019 NSSYI, presented in this report, raise questions about whether this is a focus for administrators. For instance, participants were asked to rate the extent of "the presence of experiences with diversity, wherein students are exposed to and must contend with people and circumstances that differ from those with which students are familiar." Across the overall sample, 35.6% of institutions reported that this was partially present. An additional 18.6% rated this as a 2 on the scale of 1 to 5, and 23.7% rated it as a 1, indicating that the element was largely not present within academic advising. These results spur questions, such as how might staff tailor advising practices so that all students have the resources and support they need to succeed, believe that the institution cares about them, and feel that they belong to their community? Institutional staff may also consider how advising can be used to engage students in practices and reflections that promote diversity and equity.

Lastly, we note not only that the sophomore-year experience looks different across institution types but also that students encounter these efforts in various ways. One of the limitations of the 2019 NSSYI was the small sample of community colleges. This is similar to previous administrations of the NSSYI, which have also lacked a robust community college sample (Young et al., 2015). As such, we encourage research that seeks to understand what the sophomore year might look like for community college students, including full-time and part-time students. The "sophomore year" might not be the most accurate way of framing and measuring students' progress, experiences, or success, as researchers and practitioners continue to define sophomores by the number of academic credits earned and/or the number of years a student has been enrolled in higher education (Schreiner, 2018). Additionally, existing literature and research related to sophomore students, including the NSSYI, has largely not addressed ways in which partnerships across institutional sectors may be leveraged to support students grappling with decisions associated with the sophomore year (e.g., community college students seeking to transfer to four-year schools or enter industry).

Discussion and Practical Applications

When colleges and universities identify objectives for sophomores and organize their work to deliver on those objectives, they create conditions for success. The results from the 2019 National Survey of Sophomore-Year Initiatives (NSSYI) does not uncover or present anything new in terms of objectives and initiatives associated with the sophomore year. Career exploration and planning, academic success, and identification of pathways all echo themes present in previous work on the sophomore year (Hunter et al., 2009; Schreiner, 2018). Yet the finding that nearly a third of institutions have not identified objectives for sophomores at the campuswide level indicates that there is still much work to do. This result illustrates that sophomore programs are frequently not given the institutional resources, organization, connectivity, and focus needed for them to engage students and help them connect with the campus in pursuit of academic, career, and other personal goals.

Moreover, and stated simply, the conversation about institutional integrity – that is, delivering on the explicit and implicit promises an institution makes to its students about their capability to succeed – is one about equity. When institutions abandon attention to intentionally delivering on the promise of higher education, the consequences can be serious and deleterious. These actions are particularly poignant for students from groups that have historically been disenfranchised from higher education, namely Black, Indigenous, and other minoritized people as well as populations such as students from low-income backgrounds. Recent data from the National Student Clearinghouse (2019) demonstrates that while retention and persistence rates have improved for students overall, there are still gaps among racially minoritized students. For example, one fifth of all Black students who successfully complete their first year leave before the beginning of the third (CSRDE, 2015).

Previous studies have demonstrated that when minoritized students develop a sense of belonging or a psychological sense of community, they exhibit higher levels of thriving and are more likely to persist from the second to the third year of a baccalaureate program (Golden, 2011; Petersen, 2019; Schreiner, 2018; Young et al., 2015). However, racially minoritized students frequently do not experience belonging to the same extent or in the same ways as White students (Petersen, 2019; Schreiner, 2018; Young et al., 2015). For example, among sophomores responding to the *Sophomore Experiences Survey*, White students were more likely to report a positive sense of community on campus than were Asian, Black, and Latinx students, with Asian students reporting the lowest levels (Young et al., 2015). As psychological sense of community consistently predicts overall thriving across sophomores (Young et al., 2015) and because institutional receptivity to student characteristics can contribute to student sense of belonging and retention (Blekic et al., 2019), it is imperative that institutional agents, including faculty, staff, and administrators, strive to adapt their work to engender belonging for students, particularly those from racially minoritized or socioeconomically disadvantaged backgrounds.

So, what can institutions do to better achieve institutional integrity and improve students' opportunities for success on campus? First, institutional agents must accept that when they admit students, they have a responsibility to support students' well-being holistically. This responsibility includes ensuring that students' needs are met, including their most basic physiological needs (e.g., housing, food, financial, health, safety; see Maslow, 1943; Young & Keup, 2019) as well as higher order needs, such as belonging and community in service of student learning and development.

In service of helping students feel included and supported by their college or university, Schreiner (2018) suggested that educators intentionally design the sophomore year around high-impact practices that connect students to faculty in meaningful ways. In addition, students are best served when campus efforts are focused and organized toward achieving institutional objectives, both stated and tacit. Moreover, institutions must engage in a critical review to better align their goals with student needs, expectations, and ambitions. This review is particularly important when student definitions and expectations of success vary widely, such as at broad-access and community colleges. As Goldrick-Rab (2010) stated, "descriptions of success in the community college sector must carefully define its terms and conditions and recognize the implications of metrics" (p. 439). It then follows that institutions must measure student outcomes and disaggregate them to understand how well they are supporting the success of sophomores from a variety of backgrounds, particularly minoritized and low socioeconomic-status students (Schreiner et al., 2018). This requires institutions to integrate and organize – or align – their efforts within and across activities created in service of sophomore success.

To that end, in the sections that follow, we offer perspectives based on the results presented that will position institutions of higher education to better support student success on their campuses: (a) incorporating elements of high-impact practices and (b) aligning institutional efforts, including, vertically, horizontally, and cross-functionally. Following these perspectives, we articulate how these point to directions for future research and applications in practice.

Element of High-Impact Practices: Connecting Sophomores to Social and Academic Community Through Advising

High-impact practices (HIPs) have dominated the discussion on student success since they were introduced by the Association of American Colleges and Universities (AAC&U) over a decade ago (Kuh, 2008). Many institutions have adopted HIPs, such as service learning, internships, and learning communities as sophomore-specific initiatives (Young et al., 2015). Participation in HIPs in the second year at a four-year institution has been shown to contribute to retention, even net of selection bias (Provencher & Kassel, 2019). As previously stated, there is evidence that sophomore programs may contain elements of HIPs, or characteristics that lead to the high impact found in the list of 10 practices originally put forward by AAC&U (Kuh, 2008). Moreover, we contend that the intentional incorporation of these elements into sophomore programming aimed at helping students achieve proficiency toward key developmental learning outcomes can also engender a positive sense of community on campuses.

According to data from the 2019 NSSYI, the element of HIPs most frequently identified by institutional respondents was interactions with faculty and peers around substantive matters: Eight in 10 respondents reported that element was at least partially present in their sophomore-year initiative. Faculty provide important mentorship and advising whether or not they are institutionally designated as advisors. In addition, they provide social capital, socialize students into the discipline, and assist students with social development (Center for Community College Student Engagement, 2014; Schreiner & Tobolowsky, 2018; Tovar, 2015). However, these interactions and their benefits are frequently inequitably distributed to students by campuses and institutional agents. Research has found that racially and ethnically minoritized students (e.g., Black, Asian American, and Latinx) interact infrequently with faculty and may receive little benefit from these interactions (Kim, 2010; Lundberg & Schreiner, 2004).

A lack of student interaction with faculty and staff may stem from students' uneven experiences with student-success staff, including advisors. For instance, aspirations and success for Latinx community college students have been improved by encouraging messages and support from institutional agents (Bordes-Edgar et al., 2011; Center for Community College Student Engagement, 2014; Tovar, 2015). In contrast, minoritized students may avoid interactions with faculty and staff because of previous and ongoing experiences in which institutional agents – including advisors – have been unhelpful, racially insensitive, or discriminatory (Lee, 2018). Outcomes are improved when attention is paid to the quality of the interaction (Kim & Sax, 2017), when advisors are conscious of race and racism and the role they play in the experiences of minoritized students (Lee, 2018), and when faculty foster positive classroom climates, encouraging diverse viewpoints in discussions and presenting multiple perspectives in the class (Ash & Schreiner, 2016).

Academic advising is well positioned to deliver on this and other elements of HIPs for sophomores. Not only was it the sophomore program most often named in the 2019 NSSYI as the initiative that reached the greatest proportion of students, but it was also the top response for how institutions achieved their objectives associated with the second year. The two elements of HIPs that were most frequently reported as at least partially present in sophomore advising were high performance expectations (83.1%) and interactions with faculty and peers around substantive matters (81.4%). These were followed by frequent, timely, and constructive feedback (78.0%), investment of time and effort (76.3%), opportunities to reflect and integrate learning (67.8%), and learning through real-world applications (67.8%).

Understanding how sophomore advising is organized to incorporate these elements allows those who support students to build on strengths of academic advising to help students achieve critical learning outcomes. First, feedback is critical to help students understand their progress within each learning outcome and proficiency. Second, it is important for both students and advisors to understand that an investment of time and effort in real-world applications and experiences is critical and necessary to achieve these competencies. Third, providing students the space to engage in reflection is a necessary part of the learning process. Finally, as sophomores interact with advisors – be they faculty, professional advisors, or staff serving in an advising role – around substantive academic matters, advising provides the space and the material for students to engage in integrative thinking and learning as well as deepen their academic and institutional commitment. Moreover, as the sophomore year and its associated developmental tasks frequently represent the convergence of the academic and social worlds in college (Schaller, 2010), advisors can work with students to find ways to craft experiences and deepen their participation in academic communities that allow students to thrive and achieve their goals.

Alignment: Vertical, Horizontal, and Cross-Functional

When colleges and universities identify objectives for sophomores and organize their work to deliver on those objectives, they create conditions for success. As we discussed the findings from the 2019 NSSYI, it became clear to us that for a college or university to achieve a desirable environment supportive of and responsive to sophomores, campus efforts would need to be aligned in at least three ways: vertically, horizontally, and cross-functionally.

Vertical Alignment: Sustained Support for Sophomores

Building on previous calls to integrate undergraduate baccalaureate curricula and supports for student transitions (see Barefoot et al., 2005; Boyer Commission, 1998; Scott, 2012), recent commentators have suggested that the sophomore year forms one part of a vertically aligned approach (Skipper, 2019; Young, 2016). *Vertical alignment* in this case refers to providing sustained support to students throughout their undergraduate experience. More specifically, vertical alignment calls for staff to build upon the experiences and support created during the first year of a student's program as students progress into their second year. This momentum is carried through to graduation and provides a successful platform for students (Skipper, 2019). As Skipper indicated, "the second college year is a key component in ensuring vertical alignment in the undergraduate experience" (p. 10) because it forms a bridge from the goals of the first year to the goals that institutions have for students upon graduation. When institutional staff do not intentionally align their objectives vertically, they may miss multiple opportunities to support sophomore students, including supporting career and academic planning, engaging students in high-impact practices, and cultivating a sense of belonging.

It is important for institutions to consider how objectives and support structures in the first year connect with developmentally appropriate objectives and supports in the sophomore year. There is evidence to support the idea that, in many cases, an effective institutional focus on the first-year experience has simply postponed many transition issues into the second year, leading to greater-than-expected amounts of departure (Schreiner & Tobolowsky, 2018). Additionally, Kuh et al. (2005) found that clearly marked academic pathways lead to student success. Sophomore experiences can build on efforts from the first year and be a springboard for success in the rest of the educational experience. Guided pathways, a practice that was developed and has found great success in community colleges and, recently, four-year campuses, are an example of how this kind of thinking can be made manifest in curricular spaces (American Association of Community Colleges, 2021). Giving students structure and flexibility can help them engage in exploration while still making meaningful progress toward an academic credential.

As campuses create vertically aligned initiatives, it is important to help students build self-efficacy and deeper understanding of who they are and who they are becoming. Traditional-aged sophomores (i.e., 18- to 24-year-olds) are poised to begin making academic and institutional commitments and establishing identities that start to blend their academic and social lives as they finish moving through core general education requirements. However, sophomores often experience difficulty selecting an academic major and considering and planning for a career (Gordon, 2010; Graunke & Woosley, 2005). Thus, issues of commitment, belonging, purpose, self-understanding, and identity come to the forefront. Institutional agents can normalize these matters as components of the second year through conversations and initiatives designed to help students view their current location in an educational trajectory and develop skills to navigate it.

Building on navigational capital and other knowledge (i.e., skills developed and adopted to advance through social institutions in spite of multiple barriers; Yosso, 2005) that students have developed prior to their arrival on campus – through experiences in previous educational settings, communities, and cultures – can validate racially minoritized and low-income students. For instance, research has demonstrated that communicating empowering language to Black and Latinx students in community colleges is critical in helping provide psychological support for students and working against stereotype threat, the internalized feeling that the assets students bring with them are inadequate for success (Crisp, 2010; Lee, 2018; Tovar, 2015). Institutional agents must seek to understand students through an asset-based perspective, validating students' knowledge, strengths, and experiences. When agents are aware of the roles of race, ethnicity, socioeconomic status, and family background (among other characteristics) in students' participation and experiences, faculty and staff can be more receptive and responsive to students and better aid students to achieve their academic goals.

However, the proverbial elephant in the room often not discussed as explicitly in the literature related to the sophomore year is how these issues play out in community colleges. For example, student enrollment patterns in community colleges vary widely based on students' needs, desires, and life circumstances as well as availability and timing of courses, among other factors (Center for Community College Student Engagement, 2017). Thus, sustained institutional support might need be drawn out or compressed as students move through their educational journey.

Another issue that arises when considering how to create a vertically aligned approach is student movement between institutions, such as transfer and student swirl (Johnson & Muse, 2012; Taylor & Jain, 2017). Considering vertical transfer, which is movement from a community college to a four-year institution (or vice versa), some approaches to improving vertical integration can include actionable and clear articulation agreements and transfer advising for students seeking to earn bachelor's degrees (Taylor & Jain, 2017). One promising practice includes the creation of cross-institutional partnerships that allow students to participate in the community of the receiving campus. Giving students access to academic and cocurricular activities and engagement may provide them with additional networks and peers and increased access to support services (Mangan, 2018; Mobelini, 2013). One example of such a partnership is the Mellon Pathways Program, a collaborative effort between John Tyler Community College (JTCC), J. Sargeant Reynolds Community College (JSRCC), and Virginia Commonwealth University (VCU). The Mellon Pathways Program provides prospective transfer students at JTCC and JSRCC with access to VCU faculty mentors, VCU events and social opportunities, and VCU academic and career resources (Truong, 2021; Virginia Commonwealth University, 2021).

It is also important to recognize the power dynamics at play in cross-institutional vertical alignment. Community colleges are at the behest of their four-year partners. Notably, when it comes to academic policies associated with transfer (such as admission, credit articulation, and more), receiving four-year institutions possess a predominant voice in what counts (Herrera & Jain, 2013). In many cases, the four-year institutions have no responsibility to ensure how or that efforts will align, which can have dire consequences for community college students seeking to transfer. As such, institutional agents must attend to these issues of power and prioritize solutions that facilitate the success of the students moving between campuses. For instance, institutional agents at four-year schools can recognize their responsibility in ensuring student success by establishing a transfer-receptive culture, one that defines the needs of students, commits to promoting transfer student retention, and provides services tailored toward students' goals (Herrera & Jain, 2013).

Horizontal Alignment: Connecting Objectives to Initiatives

If vertical alignment is focused on connecting objectives and initiatives in a sequenced fashion, *horizontal alignment* then refers to intentionally connecting stated objectives to initiatives. Furthermore, Young (2016) asserted that "vertical integration of transition program[s] also requires, and is built upon, horizontal alignment between objectives, the developmental needs of students, and educational environments" (p. 25). The results of the 2019 NSSYI indicate at least nominal horizontal alignment between institutional and programmatic objectives and sophomore programs. Over a third of responding institutions identified career exploration and preparation, academic planning, and academic success as key institutional objectives of the sophomore year on their campuses. The most frequently named sophomore-year initiatives on campuses were career exploration, academic advising, career planning, and academic coaching or mentoring. Similarly, this pattern is repeated when institutions identified initiatives critical to meeting the sophomore-year objectives, listing academic advising, career exploration, and career planning. These findings confirm prior research that highlights academic and career advising as significant, common, and integral to sophomore student success.

Horizontal alignment further highlights how advising is uniquely positioned to provide the kind of support needed for achieving developmental outcomes. The sophomore year presents students with many choices and opportunities designed to help them succeed and persist. It is especially important that students' choices aid in their developing purpose and commitment, thereby solidifying the work that will prepare them and set them on a trajectory of success. More than just simply selecting a major, finding purpose and making commitments is also about determining a path, gaining a clearer sense of self, and making the college experience one's own (Schaller, 2010; Schreiner, 2018). Academic and career advisors, whether institutionally designated or playing that important role, are key figures in helping deliver on the promise of horizontal alignment.

Because advising and interaction with faculty and staff is a significant, common, and integral piece of the sophomore success puzzle, it bears repeating that there is much work to do here. Research has found that sophomore student satisfaction with advising is low, largely due to its lack of connection to career planning (an issue with horizontal alignment between the activity and the institutional goals for the sophomore year) and a lack of in-depth personalized attention to students (Schreiner & Tobolowsky, 2018; Young et al., 2015). This dissatisfaction is particularly pronounced among Asian American, Black, and Latinx sophomore students (Young et al., 2015). As mentioned previously, student interactions with advisors can be uneven. Even that is a euphemism; despite evidence that Latinx and Black students from community colleges have indicated that positive interactions with staff are key components of self-efficacy and achievement, evidence suggests that interactions can have deleterious effects due to racially insensitive, discriminatory, or racist behaviors on the part of higher education professionals (Lee, 2018). When faculty and advisors have interactions that are supportive, connected to students' academic programs, focused on the student's personal development, and validating of students' identities, the expressed objectives and educational activities have better horizontal alignment. This type of interaction is also an important pathway to thriving as well as to an overall positive sense of belonging among racially and ethnically minoritized sophomores.

Cross-Functional Alignment: Coordination and Collaboration

Reports based on previous administrations of the NSSYI (2005, 2008, and 2014) pointed to academic advising as the primary sophomore-year initiative by virtue of its being named the initiative that reached the greatest proportion of sophomores by the greatest percentage of respondents (see Young et al., 2015). However, when we investigated the nature of how institutions horizontally aligned their initiatives with their institution-level sophomore objectives, we further confirmed a finding previously reported about sophomore-year initiatives: They are diffuse across a number of offices and departments on campus. To illustrate, when asked about sophomore programs that were crucial to reaching campuswide objectives, approximately 60% of institutions pointed to academic advising. Nearly 40% of institutions identified career exploration, career planning, and major exploration and selection as important initiatives. Lastly, approximately 20% of institutions in the sample noted that academic coaching or mentoring were necessary to meet their objectives related to the sophomore year. Because the percentages reporting just these five initiatives sums to more than 100%, it is clear that institutions are using multiple sophomore-year initiatives to achieve their objectives. While this result alone does not imply that these sophomore-focused initiatives are intentionally connected and coordinated, it certainly suggests that to achieve the promise of horizontal alignment, institutions should pursue *cross-functional alignment*.

Aligning sophomore success activities across campus provides several benefits. Skipper (2019) suggested that aligning efforts across functional areas is one way to address the challenges associated with bringing sophomore initiatives to scale. This is particularly important to ensure that sophomore experiences are delivered to large numbers of sophomores in equitable ways, reducing the probability that students are denied access to these programs. Similarly, engaging in alignment of sophomore programs across functional lines can put institutions in better position to help their sophomores engage in critical developmental tasks associated with this critical time in their education.

Simply put, unless there is coordination across departments and agreement about the value of sophomore student development, the approach will be fragmented, and success will be scattered across those who are working intentionally toward those goals. Moreover, it better ensures that the students receive a consistent message when they engage with faculty and staff about the issues they are facing; this, in turn, will present a consistent picture of how the institution intends to make good on the promises offered at the beginning of college and will lead to a stronger sense of community cohesion not only among the students but among those who work toward their success.

Future Directions

The research presented in this report has gone to some length to confirm what was previously known about institutional approaches to the sophomore year, as well as to provide deeper understanding of the role of academic advising for sophomores. Moreover, it has pointed to key ways to improve the practice of supporting sophomore student success. Notwithstanding, through analysis, interpretation, and discussion of the findings, we were faced with questions about how we currently understand the sophomore year and how our assumptions influence the questions we ask, the ways we conceptualize the experience, and those who are included in our definition of sophomores.

Definitional elements surrounding the sophomore year are not new (see Hunter et al., 2009), yet our current discussion has highlighted more complexity. Much of the description of the context of sophomore students and the programs designed to support them tend to assume a traditional-aged full-time sophomore. Even many of the definitional considerations (e.g., time-bound, credit-based) of the idea of the sophomore year are based on this assumption. Much of the research that describes sophomore student success is based on studies of second-year students in four-year institutions where students are more likely to be full-time, traditional-aged, and from majoritized populations. As mentioned in the previous section of this report, more work is needed to understand the experiences of post-traditional, part-time, community-college-attending sophomores. To truly achieve models of integration, agents must better understand their students and adopt sophomore-year initiatives that are flexible, hybridized, and contextualized.

Conclusion

The results from the 2019 NSSYI highlight ways in which institutions and individuals working within them can intentionally integrate their efforts in the sophomore year to support students' growth, thriving, and overall sense of belonging on campus. Whether this report is used as reference material for benchmarking, a practical guide for creating learning outcomes, or fodder for critique of how student-success programs are conceptualized and executed, it is our hope that it pushes the conversation forward for sophomore student success, particularly students from racially and ethnically minoritized and socioeconomically disadvantaged backgrounds.

Appendix A: 2019 National Survey of Sophomore-Year Initiatives

Instructions

This survey is intended to gather information regarding sophomore-year initiatives on your campus. The survey should take approximately 30-45 minutes to complete. While you may exit the survey at any time and your responses will be saved, we recommend completing the entire survey in one sitting.

Your responses are important to us, so please complete this survey by March 31, 2019. Thank you.

Specifically, you will be asked questions regarding the following:

- General institutional information
- Institutional attention to sophomores
- Coordination of institutional efforts
- Types of programs offered to sophomores
- Characteristics of the predominant sophomore-year initiative
  - Educationally effective practices
  - Administration
  - Assessment and evaluation
- Characteristics of academic advising in the sophomore year
  - Educationally effective practices
  - Administration
  - Assessment and evaluation

For the purposes of this survey, we offer the following definitions:

Campus or Institution: These terms, used interchangeably, refer to an individual campus that is either (a) an independent entity or (b) meaningfully distinct from other campuses in a system.

Sophomores: Students in their second year at the same campus (excluding transfer students). These students may not have attained official standing based on accumulated credits.

Sophomore Year: Similar to the definition of sophomore, this refers to the second year a student or a cohort of students have been at the same campus (excluding transfer students). Can be used interchangeably with second year.

45

Sophomore-Year Initiative: Any educational offering specifically or intentionally geared toward sophomore students. This goes beyond merely making educational activities available to sophomore-year students. Some sophomore-year programs may be a subset of a larger department or exist independently. For example, sophomore advising may be a clearly defined specialty and focus area in a campus advising center. However, just assigning second-year students to advisors is not, in itself, a sophomore-year program.

You can find a list of examples of sophomore-year initiatives here.

If you would like a copy of your responses, you will need to print each page of your survey before moving on to the next page.

Institutional Information

Please provide the following information:

Q1. Full name of institution: _____

   City: _____

   State: _____

   Your first name: _____

   Your last name: _____

   Your title: _____

   Your e-mail address: _____

Institutional Attention to the Sophomore Year

Q2. Which of the following campuswide objectives has your institution identified specifically for sophomores? (Select all that apply.)

- ❒ Academic planning
- ❒ Academic success strategies
- ❒ Analytical, critical-thinking, or problem-solving skills
- ❒ Career exploration and/or preparation
- ❒ Civic engagement
- ❒ Common sophomore-year experience
- ❒ Connection with the institution or campus
- ❒ Developmental education, remediation, and/or review
- ❒ Digital literacy
- ❒ Discipline-specific knowledge
- ❒ Graduate or professional school preparation (e.g., premed, prelaw)
- ❒ Health and wellness
- ❒ Information literacy
- ❒ Integrative and applied learning
- ❒ Intercultural competence, diversity skills, or engaging with different perspectives
- ❒ Introduction to a major, discipline, or career path

❑ Introduction to college-level academic expectations

❑ Introduction to the liberal arts

❑ Knowledge of institution or campus resources and services

❑ Major exploration

❑ Oral communication skills

❑ Persistence, retention, or third-year return rates

❑ Personal exploration or development

❑ Project planning, teamwork, or management skills

❑ Social support networks (e.g., friendships)

❑ Student-faculty interaction

❑ Writing skills

❑ Other, please specify: _____

❑ Our institution has not identified campuswide objectives specifically for the sophomore year.

Q3. Which of the following institutional efforts have included a specific focus on sophomores? (Select all that apply.)

❑ Accreditation (e.g., Action Project or Quality Enhancement Plan focused on sophomore-year students)

❑ Advising study

❑ Curricular or gateway course redesign

❑ Employment or job-placement study

❑ Graduation study

❑ Grant-funded project

❑ Institutional assessment

❑ Participation in a national survey of sophomore-year students (e.g., Noel-Levitz, Sophomore Experiences Survey)

❑ Pathways programs or metamajors

❑ Program self-study

❑ Retention study

❑ Strategic planning

❑ Student services programming

❑ Other, please specify: _____

❑ Our institution has not engaged in any efforts with a specific focus on the sophomore- year. *[Go to Q5]*

Q4. How long have your institutional efforts included a specific focus on sophomores?

❑ 1 year or less

❑ 2-5 years

❒   6-10 years

❒   11-15 years

❒   16-20 years

❒   more than 20 years

Current Sophomore-Year Initiatives

Q5. Does your institution currently offer any initiatives specifically or intentionally geared toward sophomore students?

❒   Yes

❒   No *[Go to Q59]*

❒   I don't know. *[Go to Q59]*

Q6. In which of the following areas does your institution currently have initiatives specifically or intentionally geared toward sophomore students? (Select all that apply.)

❒   Academic advising

❒   Academic coaching or mentoring

❒   Back-to-school events

❒   Campus-based event (e.g., common reading experiences, dinners, fairs)

❒   Career exploration

❒   Career planning

❒   Communication or publications (e.g., social media, newsletters, emails, brochures)

❒   Course-specific support for classes with high dropout, fail, or withdraw rates (e.g., Supplemental Instruction)

❒   Credit-bearing course (e.g., sophomore seminar)

❒   Cultural enrichment activities (e.g., plays, musical events, multicultural fairs)

❒   Early alert systems

❒   Faculty or staff mentors

❒   Financial aid (e.g., sophomore scholarships, loans)

❒   Internships or co-ops

❒   Leadership development

❒   Learning communities (i.e., students take two or more linked courses as a group)

❒   Major exploration and selection

❒   Off-campus event (e.g., retreat, outdoor adventure)

❒   Opportunities to co-teach or assist in teaching a class

❒   Peer mentoring by sophomores (i.e., sophomore students mentoring any other students)

❒   Peer mentors for sophomores (i.e., undergraduate students mentoring sophomores)

❒   Practica or other supervised practice experiences

❒ Residence life—sophomore live on-campus requirement

❒ Residence life—sophomore-specific living-learning community

❒ Residence life—sophomore-specific residential curriculum

❒ Service-learning or community service

❒ Student government (e.g., sophomore council)

❒ Study abroad

❒ Undergraduate research

❒ Other, please specify: _____

Coordination of Sophomore-Year Initiatives

Q7. On your campus, how coordinated are sophomore-year initiatives? (Select the most appropriate answer.)

Totally decentralized, no coordination between any departments or units in sophomore-year initiatives				Totally centralized, all sophomore-year initiatives are coordinated by a single director or office	Don't know
1	2	3	4	5	DK

[Display if Q7 = 2-4]
Q8. Which campus units participate in the coordination of their sophomore-year initiatives? (Select all that apply.)

❒ Academic advising

❒ Academic affairs central office

❒ Academic department(s), please specify: _____

❒ Career services

❒ Center for teaching excellence

❒ Enrollment management central office

❒ Residence life or housing

❒ Student activities and leadership

❒ Student affairs central office

❒ Student success center

❒ Other, please specify: _____

Q9. Is there currently an individual in charge of sophomore student programs or initiatives?

❒ Yes *[Go to Q10]*

❒ No *[Go to Q14]*

❒ I don't know. *[Go to Q14]*

[Display if Q9 = "Yes"]
Q10. What is the title of the individual who is responsible for sophomore student programs or initiatives (e.g., director, coordinator, dean of sophomore student programs)? _____

Q11. Is this position dedicated to sophomore programs and initiatives on a full-time basis (approximately 40 hours per week)?

   ❒ Yes *[Go to Q20]*

   ❒ No *[Go to Q18]*

   ❒ I don't know. *[Go to Q18]*

[Display if Q11 = "No" or "I don't know."]
Q12. Does this person have another position on campus?

   ❒ Yes *[Go to Q13]*

   ❒ No *[Go to Q14]*

   ❒ I don't know. *[Go to Q14]*

[Display if Q12 = "Yes"]
Q13. The other campus role of the director, coordinator, or dean of the sophomore initiative is as a/an: (Select all that apply.)

   ❒ Academic affairs administrator

   ❒ Adjunct or part-time faculty member

   ❒ Full-time or tenure-track faculty member

   ❒ Student affairs administrator

   ❒ Other, please specify: _____

Primary Institutional Initiative

Q14. Which of the following initiatives reaches the **highest proportion of sophomore students** at your institution? **(Select only one.)**

   ❒ Academic advising

   ❒ Academic coaching or mentoring

   ❒ Back-to-school events

   ❒ Campus-based event (e.g., common reading experiences, dinners, fairs)

   ❒ Career exploration

   ❒ Career planning

   ❒ Communication or publications (e.g., social media, newsletters, emails, brochures)

   ❒ Course-specific support for classes with high dropout, fail, or withdraw rates (e.g., Supplemental Instruction)

   ❒ Credit-bearing course (e.g., sophomore seminar)

   ❒ Cultural enrichment activities (e.g., plays, musical events, multicultural fairs)

   ❒ Early alert systems

❏ Faculty or staff mentors

❏ Financial aid (e.g., sophomore scholarships, loans)

❏ Internships or co-ops

❏ Leadership development

❏ Learning communities (i.e., students take two or more linked courses as a group)

❏ Major exploration and selection

❏ Off-campus event (e.g., retreat, outdoor adventure)

❏ Opportunities to co-teach or assist in teaching a class

❏ Peer mentoring by sophomores (i.e., sophomore students mentoring any other students)

❏ Peer mentors for sophomores (i.e., undergraduate students mentoring sophomores)

❏ Practica or other supervised practice experiences

❏ Residence life—sophomore live on-campus requirement

❏ Residence life—sophomore-specific living-learning community

❏ Residence life—sophomore-specific residential curriculum

❏ Service-learning or community service

❏ Student government (e.g., sophomore council)

❏ Study abroad

❏ Undergraduate research

❏ Other, please specify: _____

Q15. Which of the following are the primary sophomore-year programs by which the campuswide objectives for sophomores are met? (Please select up to 5.)

❏ Academic advising

❏ Academic coaching or mentoring

❏ Back-to-school events

❏ Campus-based event (e.g., common reading experiences, dinners, fairs)

❏ Career exploration

❏ Career planning

❏ Communication or publications (e.g., social media, newsletters, emails, brochures)

❏ Course-specific support for classes with high dropout, fail, or withdraw rates (e.g., Supplemental Instruction)

❏ Credit-bearing course (e.g., sophomore seminar)

❏ Cultural enrichment activities (e.g., plays, musical events, multicultural fairs)

❏ Early alert systems

❏ Faculty or staff mentors

❏ Financial aid (e.g., sophomore scholarships, loans)

❏ Internships or co-ops

❐ Leadership development

❐ Learning communities (i.e., students take two or more linked courses as a group)

❐ Major exploration and selection

❐ Off-campus event (e.g., retreat, outdoor adventure)

❐ Opportunities to co-teach or assist in teaching a class

❐ Peer mentoring by sophomores (i.e., sophomore students mentoring any other students)

❐ Peer mentors for sophomores (i.e., undergraduate students mentoring sophomores)

❐ Practica or other supervised practice experiences

❐ Residence life—sophomore live on-campus requirement

❐ Residence life—sophomore-specific living-learning community

❐ Residence life—sophomore-specific residential curriculum

❐ Service-learning or community service

❐ Student government (e.g., sophomore council)

❐ Study abroad

❐ Undergraduate research

❐ Other, please specify: _____

[If response to Q14 is anything other than "Academic Advising", participants will respond to Q16-Q35]
You indicated the initiative reaching the highest proportion of sophomore students on your campus is [Insert response from Q14]. Please answer the following questions based only on this initiative.
[To be repeated at the beginning of each page]

The Students

Q16. What is the approximate percentage of sophomore students this initiative reaches on your campus?

❐ 10% or less

❐ 11-20%

❐ 21-30%

❐ 31-40%

❐ 41-50%

❐ 51-60%

❐ 61-70%

❐ 71-80%

❐ 81-90%

❐ 91-100%

Q17. What proportion of your sophomore students are required to participate in this initiative?

❏ None are required to participate *[Go to Question 19]*

❏ Less than 10%

❏ 10-19%

❏ 20-29%

❏ 30-39%

❏ 40-49%

❏ 50-59%

❏ 60-69%

❏ 70-79%

❏ 80-89%

❏ 90-99%

❏ 100% - All sophomore students are required to participate *[Go to Question19]*

Q18. Which of the following groups of sophomore students are required to participate in this initiative? (Select all that apply.)

❏ Academically underprepared students

❏ First-generation students

❏ Honors students

❏ International students

❏ Learning community participants

❏ Preprofessional students (e.g., prelaw, premed)

❏ Student athletes

❏ Students enrolled in developmental or remedial courses

❏ Students on probationary status

❏ Students residing within a particular residence hall

❏ Students with fewer credits than necessary for sophomore status

❏ Students within specific majors, please list:_____

❏ TRIO participants

❏ Undeclared students

❏ Other, please specify: _____

Q19. Which of the following groups of sophomore students are specifically targeted by this initiative? (Select all that apply.)

❏ Academically underprepared students

❏ First-generation students

❏ Honors students

❏ International students

❐ Learning community participants

❐ Preprofessional students (e.g., prelaw, premed)

❐ Student athletes

❐ Students enrolled in developmental or remedial courses

❐ Students on probationary status

❐ Students residing within a particular residence hall

❐ Students with fewer credits than necessary for sophomore status

❐ Students within specific majors, please list:_____

❐ TRIO participants

❐ Undeclared students

❐ Other, please specify: _____

❐ No sophomore students are specifically targeted by this initiative.

Characteristics of the Initiative

Q20. How long has this initiative been in place?

❐ 2 years or less

❐ 3-5 years

❐ 6-10 years

❐ 11-15 years

❐ 16-20 years

❐ More than 20 years

Q21. Please select the **three** most important objectives for this initiative:

❐ Academic planning

❐ Academic success strategies

❐ Analytical, critical-thinking, or problem-solving skills

❐ Career exploration and/or preparation

❐ Civic engagement

❐ Common sophomore-year experience

❐ Connection with the institution or campus

❐ Developmental education, remediation, and/or review

❐ Digital literacy

❐ Discipline-specific knowledge

❐ Graduate or professional school preparation (e.g., premed, prelaw)

❐ Health and wellness

❐ Information literacy

❐ Integrative and applied learning

❏ Intercultural competence, diversity skills, or engaging with different perspectives

❏ Introduction to a major, discipline, or career path

❏ Introduction to college-level academic expectations

❏ Introduction to the liberal arts

❏ Knowledge of institution or campus resources and services

❏ Major exploration

❏ Oral communication skills

❏ Persistence, retention, or third-year return rates

❏ Personal exploration or development

❏ Project planning, teamwork, or management skills

❏ Social support networks (e.g., friendships)

❏ Student-faculty interaction

❏ Writing skills

❏ Other, please specify: _____

Educationally Effective Practices

Q22-29. To what extent are each of the following elements present in this initiative?

Element	Element is not present 1	2	Element is partially present 3	4	Element is pervasive throughout initiative 5
Performance expectations set at appropriately high levels					
Significant investment of time and effort by students over an extended period of time					
Interactions with faculty and peers about substantive matters					
Experiences with diversity, wherein students are exposed to and must contend with people and circumstances that differ from those with which students are familiar					
Frequent, timely, and constructive feedback					
Periodic, structured opportunities to reflect and integrate learning					
Opportunities to discover relevance of learning through real-world applications					
Public demonstration of competence					

Administration of the Initiative

Q30. Which campus unit directly administers this initiative?

☐ Academic affairs central office

☐ Academic department(s), please list: _____

☐ College or school (e.g., College of Liberal Arts)

☐ Sophomore-year program office

☐ Student affairs central office

❐ University college

❐ Other, please specify: _____

Q31. How is the initiative primarily funded?

❐ Auxiliary funds—non-tuition-based fees and services (e.g., housing, bookstore)

❐ Foundation funds

❐ Grant funds

❐ Nonrecurring or one-time funds

❐ Recurring state- or university-appropriated funds

❐ Student activity fees

❐ Tuition revenue

❐ Other, please specify: _____

Assessment and Evaluation

Q32. Has this initiative been formally assessed or evaluated in the past three years?

❐ Yes *[Go to Q33]*

❐ No *[Go to Q35]*

❐ I don't know. *[Go to Q35]*

[Display if Q32 = "Yes"]
Q33. What type of assessment was conducted? (Select all that apply.)

❐ Analysis of institutional data (e.g., GPA, retention rates, graduation)

❐ Direct assessment of student learning outcomes

❐ Focus groups with faculty

❐ Focus groups with professional staff

❐ Focus groups with students

❐ Individual interviews with faculty

❐ Individual interviews with orientation staff

❐ Individual interviews with students

❐ Program review

❐ Student course evaluation

❐ Survey instrument *[Go to Q35]*

❐ Other, please specify: _____

[Display if Q33 = "Direct assessment of student learning outcomes"]
Q34. Please identify the student learning outcomes you assessed: (Select all that apply.)

❐ Academic planning

❐ Academic success strategies

❐ Analytical, critical-thinking, or problem-solving skills

- ❏ Career exploration and/or preparation
- ❏ Civic engagement
- ❏ Common sophomore-year experience
- ❏ Connection with the institution or campus
- ❏ Developmental education, remediation, and/or review
- ❏ Digital literacy
- ❏ Discipline-specific knowledge
- ❏ Graduate or professional school preparation (e.g., premed, prelaw)
- ❏ Health and wellness
- ❏ Information literacy
- ❏ Integrative and applied learning
- ❏ Intercultural competence, diversity skills, or engaging with different perspectives
- ❏ Introduction to a major, discipline, or career path
- ❏ Introduction to college-level academic expectations
- ❏ Introduction to the liberal arts
- ❏ Knowledge of institution or campus resources and services
- ❏ Major exploration
- ❏ Oral communication skills
- ❏ Persistence, retention, or third-year return rates
- ❏ Personal exploration or development
- ❏ Project planning, teamwork, or management skills
- ❏ Social support networks (e.g., friendships)
- ❏ Student-faculty interaction
- ❏ Writing skills
- ❏ Other, please specify: _____

[Display if Q33 = "Survey instrument"]
Q35. Please identify the national survey(s) you used: (Select all that apply.)

- ❏ College Student Experiences Questionnaire (CSEQ)
- ❏ Collegiate Learning Assessment (CLA)
- ❏ Community College Survey of Student Engagement (CCSSE)
- ❏ Diverse Learning Environments Survey (DLE; Administered by HERI at UCLA)
- ❏ Faculty Survey of Student Engagement (FSSE)
- ❏ Individual Developmental and Educational Assessment (IDEA)
- ❏ National Survey of Student Engagement (NSSE)
- ❏ Second-Year Student Assessment (Noel-Levitz)

- ❐ Sophomore Experiences Survey (www.thrivingincollege.org)
- ❐ Student Satisfaction Inventory (SSI)
- ❐ Other, please specify: _____

Academic Advising in the Sophomore Year

The Students

[Display if Q14 = Academic advising]
Q36. What is the approximate percentage of sophomore students reached by academic advising for sophomores on your campus?

- ❐ 10% or less
- ❐ 11-20%
- ❐ 21-30%
- ❐ 31-40%
- ❐ 41-50%
- ❐ 51-60%
- ❐ 61-70%
- ❐ 71-80%
- ❐ 81-90%
- ❐ 91-100%

Q37. What proportion of your sophomore students are required to participate in academic advising?

- ❐ None are required to participate *[Go to Q39]*
- ❐ Less than 10%
- ❐ 10-19%
- ❐ 20-29%
- ❐ 30-39%
- ❐ 40-49%
- ❐ 50-59%
- ❐ 60-69%
- ❐ 70-79%
- ❐ 80-89%
- ❐ 90-99%
- ❐ 100% - All sophomore students are required to participate *[Go to Q39]*

[Display if Q37 is not "None" or "100%]
Q38. Which of the following groups of sophomore students are **required** to participate in academic advising? (Select all that apply.)

- ❏ Academically underprepared students
- ❏ First-generation students
- ❏ Honors students
- ❏ International students
- ❏ Learning community participants
- ❏ Preprofessional students (e.g., prelaw, premed)
- ❏ Student athletes
- ❏ Students enrolled in developmental or remedial courses
- ❏ Students on probationary status
- ❏ Students residing within a particular residence hall
- ❏ Students with fewer credits than necessary for sophomore status
- ❏ Students within specific majors, please list: _____
- ❏ TRIO participants
- ❏ Undeclared students
- ❏ Other, please specify: _____

[Display if Q14 = Academic advising]
Q39. Which of the following groups of sophomore students are specifically targeted by academic advising for sophomores? (Select all that apply.)

- ❏ All sophomore students
- ❏ Academically underprepared students
- ❏ First-generation students
- ❏ Honors students
- ❏ International students
- ❏ Learning community participants
- ❏ Preprofessional students (e.g., prelaw, premed)
- ❏ Student athletes
- ❏ Students enrolled in developmental or remedial courses
- ❏ Students on probationary status
- ❏ Students residing within a particular residence hall
- ❏ Students with fewer credits than necessary for sophomore status
- ❏ Students within specific majors, please list:_____
- ❏ TRIO participants
- ❏ Undeclared students

❏ Other, please specify: _____

❏ No sophomore students are specifically targeted by academic advising.

Characteristics of the Initiative

[Display if Q14 = Academic advising]
Q40. How long has academic advising for sophomores been in place?

❏ 2 years or less

❏ 3-5 years

❏ 6-10 years

❏ 11-15 years

❏ 16-20 years

❏ More than 20 years

Q41. Please select the **three** most important objectives for academic advising in the sophomore year:

❏ Academic planning

❏ Academic success strategies

❏ Analytical, critical-thinking, or problem-solving skills

❏ Career exploration and/or preparation

❏ Civic engagement

❏ Common sophomore-year experience

❏ Connection with the institution or campus

❏ Developmental education, remediation, and/or review

❏ Digital literacy

❏ Discipline-specific knowledge

❏ Graduate or professional school preparation (e.g., premed, prelaw)

❏ Health and wellness

❏ Information literacy

❏ Integrative and applied learning

❏ Intercultural competence, diversity skills, or engaging with different perspectives

❏ Introduction to a major, discipline, or career path

❏ Introduction to college-level academic expectations

❏ Introduction to the liberal arts

❏ Knowledge of institution or campus resources and services

❏ Major exploration

❏ Oral communication skills

❏ Persistence, retention, or third-year return rates

❏ Personal exploration or development

❒ Project planning, teamwork, or management skills

❒ Social support networks (e.g., friendships)

❒ Student-faculty interaction

❒ Writing skills

❒ Other, please specify: _____

Educationally Effective Practices

[Display if Q14 = Academic advising]

Q42-49. To what extent are each of the following elements present in academic advising for sophomores?

Element	Element is not present 1	2	Element is partially present 3	4	Element is pervasive throughout initiative 5
Performance expectations set at appropriately high levels					
Significant investment of time and effort by students over an extended period of time					
Interactions with faculty and peers about substantive matters					
Experiences with diversity, wherein students are exposed to and must contend with people and circumstances that differ from those with which students are familiar					
Frequent, timely, and constructive feedback					
Periodic, structured opportunities to reflect and integrate learning					
Opportunities to discover relevance of learning through real-world applications					
Public demonstration of competence					

Administration of the Initiative

Q50. Which campus unit directly administers academic advising for sophomores?

- ❏ Academic affairs central office
- ❏ Academic department(s) (please list)
- ❏ College or school (e.g., College of Liberal Arts)
- ❏ Sophomore-year program office
- ❏ Student affairs central office
- ❏ University college
- ❏ Other, please specify: _____

Q51. How is academic advising for sophomores primarily funded?

- ❏ Auxiliary funds—non-tuition-based fees and services (e.g., housing, bookstore)
- ❏ Foundation funds
- ❏ Grant funds
- ❏ Nonrecurring or one-time funds
- ❏ Recurring state- or university-appropriated funds
- ❏ Student activity fees
- ❏ Tuition revenue
- ❏ Other, please specify: _____

Q52. Please identify the **activities and processes related to academic advising** in which your institution is currently engaged. (Select all that apply.)

- ❏ Campuswide assessment and planning
- ❏ Evaluation and continuous improvement of advising
- ❏ Leadership and change management
- ❏ Ongoing professional development and training for advisors
- ❏ Process mapping
- ❏ Structure redesign
- ❏ Technology and data governance and management
- ❏ Technology selection
- ❏ Other, please specify: _____

[Display if Q52 = "Technology selection"]
Q53. What technology tools has your institution invested in to support advising?

_____

Q54. In which of the following activities and processes related to academic advising is your institution engaged in external coaching, consultation, and training?

❐ Campuswide assessment and planning

❐ Evaluation and continuous improvement of advising

❐ Leadership and change management

❐ Ongoing professional development and training for advisors

❐ Process mapping

❐ Structure redesign

❐ Technology and data governance and management

❐ Technology selection

❐ Other, please specify: _____

Assessment and Evaluation

Q55. Has academic advising for sophomores been formally assessed or evaluated in the past three years?

❐ Yes *[Go to Q56]*

❐ No *[Go to Q57]*

❐ I don't know. *[Go to Q57]*

Q56. What type of assessment was conducted? (Select all that apply.)

❐ Analysis of institutional data (e.g., GPA, retention rates, graduation)

❐ Direct assessment of student learning outcomes *[Go to Question Q57]*

❐ Focus groups with faculty

❐ Focus groups with professional staff

❐ Focus groups with students

❐ Individual interviews with faculty

❐ Individual interviews with orientation staff

❐ Individual interviews with students

❐ Program review

❐ Student course evaluation

❐ Survey instrument *[Go to Question Q58]*

❐ Other, please specify: _____

[Display if Q56 = "Direct assessment of student learning outcomes"]
Q57. Please identify the student learning outcomes you assessed: (Select all that apply.)

❐ Academic planning

❐ Academic success strategies

❐ Analytical, critical-thinking, or problem-solving skills

❐ Career exploration and/or preparation

- ❒ Civic engagement
- ❒ Common sophomore-year experience
- ❒ Connection with the institution or campus
- ❒ Developmental education, remediation, and/or review
- ❒ Digital literacy
- ❒ Discipline-specific knowledge
- ❒ Graduate or professional school preparation (e.g., premed, prelaw)
- ❒ Health and wellness
- ❒ Information literacy
- ❒ Integrative and applied learning
- ❒ Intercultural competence, diversity skills, or engaging with different perspectives
- ❒ Introduction to a major, discipline, or career path
- ❒ Introduction to college-level academic expectations
- ❒ Introduction to the liberal arts
- ❒ Knowledge of institution or campus resources and services
- ❒ Major exploration
- ❒ Oral communication skills
- ❒ Persistence, retention, or third-year return rates
- ❒ Personal exploration or development
- ❒ Project planning, teamwork, or management skills
- ❒ Social support networks (e.g., friendships)
- ❒ Student-faculty interaction
- ❒ Writing skills
- ❒ Other, please specify: _____

[Display if Q56 = "Survey instrument"]
Q58. Please identify the national survey(s) you used: (Select all that apply.)

- ❒ College Student Experiences Questionnaire (CSEQ)
- ❒ Collegiate Learning Assessment (CLA)
- ❒ Community College Survey of Student Engagement (CCSSE)
- ❒ Diverse Learning Environments Survey (DLE; Administered by HERI at UCLA)
- ❒ Faculty Survey of Student Engagement (FSSE)
- ❒ Individual Developmental and Educational Assessment (IDEA)
- ❒ National Survey of Student Engagement (NSSE)
- ❒ Second-Year Student Assessment (Noel-Levitz)
- ❒ Sophomore Experiences Survey (www.thrivingincollege.org)

❐ Student Satisfaction Inventory (SSI)

❐ Other, please specify: _____

Past Sophomore-Year Initiatives

Q59. If your institution does not have a sophomore initiative, indicate the reason(s) why: (Select all that apply.)

❐ Lack of expertise

❐ Lack of funding

❐ Lack of staff or faculty buy-in

❐ Limited time

❐ Not an institutional priority

❐ Other, please specify: _____

Q60. Has your institution had initiatives specifically or intentionally geared toward sophomore students in the past five years?

❐ Yes [Go to Q67]

❐ No [Go to Q68]

❐ I don't know. [Go to Q68]

Q61. If yes, what were the sophomore-year initiatives? (Select all that apply.)

❐ Academic advising

❐ Academic coaching or mentoring

❐ Back-to-school events

❐ Campus-based event (e.g., common reading experiences, dinners, fairs)

❐ Career exploration

❐ Career planning

❐ Communication or publications (e.g., social media, newsletters, emails, brochures)

❐ Course-specific support for classes with high dropout, fail, or withdraw rates (e.g., Supplemental Instruction)

❐ Credit-bearing course (e.g., sophomore seminar)

❐ Cultural enrichment activities (e.g., plays, musical events, multicultural fairs)

❐ Early alert systems

❐ Faculty or staff mentors

❐ Financial aid (e.g., sophomore scholarships, loans)

❐ Internships or co-ops

❐ Leadership development

❐ Learning communities (i.e., students take two or more linked courses as a group)

❐ Major exploration and selection

❐ Off-campus event (e.g., retreat, outdoor adventure)

❒ Opportunities to co-teach or assist in teaching a class

❒ Peer mentoring by sophomores (i.e., sophomore students mentoring any other students)

❒ Peer mentors for sophomores (i.e., undergraduate students mentoring sophomores)

❒ Practica or other supervised practice experiences

❒ Residence life—sophomore live on-campus requirement

❒ Residence life—sophomore-specific living-learning community

❒ Residence life—sophomore-specific residential curriculum

❒ Service-learning or community service

❒ Student government (e.g., sophomore council)

❒ Study abroad

❒ Undergraduate research

❒ Other, please specify: _____

Future Sophomore-Year Initiatives

Q62. Is your institution considering or developing any future initiatives specifically or intentionally geared toward sophomore students?

❒ Yes *[Go to Q63]*

❒ No *[Go to Q64]*

❒ I don't know. *[Go to Q64]*

Q63. If yes, please indicate which of the following future sophomore initiative(s) your institution is considering or developing: (Select all that apply.)

❒ Academic advising

❒ Academic coaching or mentoring

❒ Back-to-school events

❒ Campus-based event (e.g., common reading experiences, dinners, fairs)

❒ Career exploration

❒ Career planning

❒ Communication or publications (e.g., social media, newsletters, emails, brochures)

❒ Course-specific support for classes with high dropout, fail, or withdraw rates (e.g., Supplemental Instruction)

❒ Credit-bearing course (e.g., sophomore seminar)

❒ Cultural enrichment activities (e.g., plays, musical events, multicultural fairs)

❒ Early alert systems

❒ Faculty or staff mentors

❒ Financial aid (e.g., sophomore scholarships, loans)

❒ Internships or co-ops

❒ Leadership development

❐ Learning communities (i.e., students take two or more linked courses as a group)

❐ Major exploration and selection

❐ Off-campus event (e.g., retreat, outdoor adventure)

❐ Opportunities to co-teach or assist in teaching a class

❐ Peer mentoring by sophomores (i.e., sophomore students mentoring any other students)

❐ Peer mentors for sophomores (i.e., undergraduate students mentoring sophomores)

❐ Practica or other supervised practice experiences

❐ Residence life—sophomore live on-campus requirement

❐ Residence life—sophomore-specific living-learning community

❐ Residence life—sophomore-specific residential curriculum

❐ Service-learning or community service

❐ Student government (e.g., sophomore council)

❐ Study abroad

❐ Undergraduate research

❐ Other, please specify: _____

Information

Q64. It is our practice to make available specific and general information gathered from this survey. In general, findings from the survey are reported in aggregate, but we may identify individual institutions that have agreed to allow their responses to be shared. Please select your preference:

❐ You may share my school's name and survey responses.

❐ You may share my school's name as a participant in the survey, but you may not share my survey responses in connection with my school's name

❐ Please do not share my school's name.

Q65. It is our practice to create a research report based on an analysis of the general information gathered from this survey. Would you like to be informed when this research report is made available?

❐ Yes

❐ No

Appendix B: List of Institutions Participating in the 2019 National Survey of Sophomore-Year Initiatives[1]

Institution	City	State
Agnes Scott College	Decatur	GA
Alabama State University	Montgomery	AL
Albertus Magnus College	New Haven	CT
Albion College	Albion	MI
Alexandria Technical & Community College	Alexandria	MN
Allen County Community College	Iola	KS
Allen University	Columbia	SC
Arkansas State University Mid-South	West Memphis	AR
Arkansas State University-Main Campus	Jonesboro	AR
Arkansas State University-Newport	Newport	AR
Baldwin Wallace University	Berea	OH
Baptist Memorial College of Health Sciences	Memphis	TN
Bellarmine University	Louisville	KY
Bemidji State University	Bemidji	MN
Bennett College	Greensboro	NC
Brandeis University	Waltham	MA
Brigham Young University-Hawaii	Laie	HI
Brigham Young University-Provo	Provo	UT
Bristol Community College	Fall River	MA
Buena Vista University	Storm Lake	IA
Caldwell Community College and Technical Institute	Hudson	NC
Caldwell University	Caldwell	NJ
California Baptist University	Riverside	CA

Table continues on page 70

[1] This is a partial list ($n = 228$) of total respondents to the National Survey of Sophomore-Year Initiatives ($N = 308$). Institutions could opt out of being publicly identified as a survey respondent.

Table continued from page 69

Institution	City	State
California State University-Bakersfield	Bakersfield	CA
California State University-East Bay	Hayward	CA
California State University-Northridge	Northridge	CA
California State University-Sacramento	Sacramento	CA
California State University-Stanislaus	Turlock	CA
Carleton College	Northfield	MN
Carroll Community College	Westminster	MD
Cedar Crest College	Allentown	PA
Cedarville University	Cedarville	OH
Central Connecticut State University	New Britain	CT
Central Piedmont Community College	Charlotte	NC
Charles R Drew University of Medicine and Science	Los Angeles	CA
Chatham University	Pittsburgh	PA
Chipola College	Marianna	FL
Christopher Newport University	Newport News	VA
City Colleges of Chicago-Wilbur Wright College	Chicago	IL
College of Biblical Studies-Houston	Houston	TX
College of Charleston	Charleston	SC
College of the Mainland	Texas City	TX
College of the Marshall Islands	Majuro	MH
College of the Ouachitas	Malvern	AR
College of William and Mary	Williamsburg	VA
Colorado College	Colorado Springs	CO
Columbia College	Columbia	SC
Community College of Allegheny County	Pittsburgh	PA
Community College of Aurora	Aurora	CO
Danville Area Community College	Danville	IL
Diablo Valley College	Pleasant Hill	CA
Duquesne University	Pittsburgh	PA
East Carolina University	Greenville	NC
Emerson College	Boston	MA
Emmanuel College	Franklin Springs	GA
Escuela de Artes Plasticas y Diseno de Puerto Rico	San Juan	PR
Estrella Mountain Community College	Avondale	AZ
Fayetteville Technical Community College	Fayetteville	NC
Ferrum College	Ferrum	VA
Fisher College	Boston	MA
Florida Agricultural and Mechanical University	Tallahassee	FL
Florida Institute of Technology	Melbourne	FL

Table continues on page 71

Table continued from page 70

Institution	City	State
Florida National University-Main Campus	Hialeah	FL
Florida State University	Tallahassee	FL
Fort Peck Community College	Poplar	MT
Framingham State University	Framingham	MA
Furman University	Greenville	SC
Gallaudet University	Washington	DC
Georgia College & State University	Milledgeville	GA
Georgia Southern University	Statesboro	GA
Germanna Community College	Locust Grove	VA
Gordon College	Wenham	MA
Governors State University	University Park	IL
Grace College and Theological Seminary	Winona Lake	IN
Grinnell College	Grinnell	IA
Heidelberg University	Tiffin	OH
Houston Baptist University	Houston	TX
Husson University	Bangor	ME
IBMC College	Fort Collins	CO
Indiana State University	Terre Haute	IN
Indiana University-East	Richmond	IN
Indiana University-Purdue University-Indianapolis	Indianapolis	IN
Iona College	New Rochelle	NY
Ivy Tech Community College	Indianapolis	IN
Jacksonville State University	Jacksonville	AL
Kansas State University	Manhattan	KS
Laguna College of Art and Design	Laguna Beach	CA
Lamar Institute of Technology	Beaumont	TX
Lamar University	Beaumont	TX
Lee University	Cleveland	TN
Lehigh University	Bethlehem	PA
Lenoir-Rhyne University	Hickory	NC
Lincoln University	Lincoln University	PA
Lindenwood University	Saint Charles	MO
Los Angeles Harbor College	Wilmington	CA
Louisiana State University-Shreveport	Shreveport	LA
Loyola Marymount University	Los Angeles	CA
Luther College	Decorah	IA
Lyon College	Batesville	AR
Malone University	Canton	OH
Manchester Community College	Manchester	CT

Table continues on page 72

Table continued from page 71

Institution	City	State
Maryville College	Maryville	TN
McKendree University	Lebanon	IL
Meredith College	Raleigh	NC
Milwaukee Institute of Art & Design	Milwaukee	WI
Missouri State University-Springfield	Springfield	MO
Missouri Western State University	Saint Joseph	MO
Nash Community College	Rocky Mount	NC
National University College	Bayamon	PR
Nebraska Indian Community College	Macy	NE
New Jersey City University	Jersey City	NJ
New York University	New York	NY
Newman University	Wichita	KS
Nicholls State University	Thibodaux	LA
North Iowa Area Community College	Mason City	IA
Northeastern State University	Tahlequah	OK
Northern New Mexico College	Espanola	NM
Northern Vermont University	Johnson	VT
NorthWest Arkansas Community College	Bentonville	AR
Northwestern College	Orange City	IA
Northwood University	Midland	MI
Norwich University	Northfield	VT
Ohio State University-Main Campus	Columbus	OH
Ohio University-Main Campus	Athens	OH
Orange Coast College	Costa Mesa	CA
Pace University	New York	NY
Pasadena City College	Pasadena	CA
Pennsylvania College of Technology	Williamsport	PA
Pennsylvania State University-Penn State DuBois	DuBois	PA
Pensacola State College	Pensacola	FL
Philander Smith College	Little Rock	AR
Pierpont Community and Technical College	Fairmont	WV
Pine Manor College	Chestnut Hill	MA
Pittsburg State University	Pittsburg	KS
Rhode Island School of Design	Providence	RI
Rivier University	Nashua	NH
Rutgers University-Camden	Camden	NJ
Sacred Heart University	Fairfield	CT
Saint Edward's University	Austin	TX
Saint John Fisher College	Rochester	NY

Table continues on page 73

Table continued from page 72

Institution	City	State
Saint Joseph's College of Maine	Standish	ME
Saint Joseph's University	Philadelphia	PA
Saint Martin's University	Lacey	WA
Salisbury University	Salisbury	MD
Sam Houston State University	Huntsville	TX
Seattle Central College	Seattle	WA
Siena College	Loudonville	NY
Siena Heights University	Adrian	MI
Simpson College	Indianola	IA
Southern Technical College	Fort Myers	FL
SOWELA Technical Community College	Lake Charles	LA
Spelman College	Atlanta	GA
St Bonaventure University	Saint Bonaventure	NY
St Lawrence University	Canton	NY
St. Mary's College of Maryland	St. Mary's City	MD
Stockton University	Galloway	NJ
Suffolk University	Boston	MA
SUNY at Albany	Albany	NY
SUNY College at Oswego	Oswego	NY
SUNY Cortland	Cortland	NY
SUNY Maritime College	Throggs Neck	NY
Susquehanna University	Selinsgrove	PA
Texas A & M International University	Laredo	TX
Texas Christian University	Fort Worth	TX
Texas State University	San Marcos	TX
Texas Woman's University	Denton	TX
The Evergreen State College	Olympia	WA
The University of Tennessee-Knoxville	Knoxville	TN
The University of Texas at Austin	Austin	TX
The University of Texas at El Paso	El Paso	TX
The University of Texas Rio Grande Valley	Edinburg	TX
Tougaloo College	Tougaloo	MS
Trinity Christian College	Palos Heights	IL
Troy University	Troy	AL
Tulane University of Louisiana	New Orleans	LA
University of Alabama at Birmingham	Birmingham	AL
University of Bridgeport	Bridgeport	CT
University of California-Berkeley	Berkeley	CA
University of Central Florida	Orlando	FL

Table continues on page 74

Table continued from page 73

Institution	City	State
University of Central Missouri	Warrensburg	MO
University of Delaware	Newark	DE
University of Guam	Mangilao	GU
University of Hartford	West Hartford	CT
University of Hawaii at Hilo	Hilo	HI
University of Houston-Clear Lake	Houston	TX
University of Houston-Downtown	Houston	TX
University of Houston-Victoria	Victoria	TX
University of Kansas	Lawrence	KS
University of Louisiana at Lafayette	Lafayette	LA
University of Louisville	Louisville	KY
University of Memphis	Memphis	TN
University of Minnesota-Rochester	Rochester	MN
University of Minnesota-Twin Cities	Minneapolis	MN
University of Nevada-Las Vegas	Las Vegas	NV
University of New England	Biddeford	ME
University of North Texas	Denton	TX
University of Northern Iowa	Cedar Falls	IA
University of Phoenix-Virginia	Glen Allen	VA
University of Richmond	University of Richmond	VA
University of San Diego	San Diego	CA
University of South Alabama	Mobile	AL
University of South Carolina-Beaufort	Bluffton	SC
University of South Carolina-Columbia	Columbia	SC
University of South Florida-St Petersburg	St. Petersburg	FL
University of St Thomas	Saint Paul	MN
University of the West	Rosemead	CA
University of Toledo	Toledo	OH
University of Utah	Salt Lake City	UT
University of Vermont	Burlington	VT
University of Wisconsin-La Crosse	La Crosse	WI
University of Wyoming	Laramie	WY
Ursuline College	Pepper Pike	OH
Villanova University	Villanova	PA
Virginia Commonwealth University	Richmond	VA
Virginia Polytechnic Institute and State University	Blacksburg	VA
Viterbo University	La Crosse	WI
Volunteer State Community College	Gallatin	TN

Table continues on page 75

Table continued from page 74

Institution	City	State
Webb Institute	Glen Cove	NY
West Virginia University at Parkersburg	Parkersburg	WV
Western State Colorado University	Gunnison	CO
Western Texas College	Snyder	TX
Westfield State University	Westfield	MA
Wichita State University	Wichita	KS
Widener University	Chester	PA
William Jessup University	Rocklin	CA
Williamson College of the Trades	Media	PA
Worcester Polytechnic Institute	Worcester	MA
Yuba College	Marysville	CA

Appendix C: Response Frequencies from the 2019 National Survey of Sophomore-Year Initiatives

Q2. Which of the following campus-wide objectives has your institution identified specifically for sophomores? (Select all that apply.)

Survey question/ responses	Institutional type				Institution control				Number of undergraduates enrolled										Total	
	Two-year		Four-year		Public		Private		Fewer than 1,000		1,001-2,500		2,501-5,000		5,001-10,000		More than 10,000			
	Freq.	%	Freq.	%	Freq.	%	Freq.	%	Freq.	%	Freq.	%	Freq.	%	Freq.	%	Freq.	%	Freq.	%
Academic planning	20	40.0%	108	41.9%	69	42.3%	55	39.9%	15	34.1%	34	47.9%	24	38.1%	21	33.3%	34	50.7%	128	41.6%
Academic success strategies	11	22.0%	99	38.4%	58	35.6%	48	34.8%	17	38.6%	22	31.0%	20	31.7%	19	30.2%	32	47.8%	110	35.7%
Analytical, critical-thinking, or problem-solving skills	9	18.0%	43	16.7%	23	14.1%	26	18.8%	8	18.2%	13	18.3%	9	14.3%	7	11.1%	15	22.4%	52	16.9%
Career exploration and/or preparation	18	36.0%	133	51.6%	77	47.2%	72	52.2%	20	45.5%	40	56.3%	25	39.7%	26	41.3%	40	59.7%	151	49.0%
Civic engagement	3	6.0%	53	20.5%	31	19.0%	25	18.1%	5	11.4%	11	15.5%	11	17.5%	10	15.9%	19	28.4%	56	18.2%
Common sophomore-year experience	2	4.0%	52	20.2%	21	12.9%	32	23.2%	5	11.4%	17	23.9%	9	14.3%	11	17.5%	12	17.9%	54	17.5%
Connection with the institution or campus	7	14.0%	83	32.2%	48	29.4%	41	29.7%	9	20.5%	19	26.8%	14	22.2%	20	31.7%	28	41.8%	90	29.2%
Developmental education, remediation, and/or review	2	4.0%	12	4.7%	5	3.1%	7	5.1%	2	4.5%	4	5.6%	4	6.3%	2	3.2%	2	3.0%	14	4.5%
Digital literacy	3	6.0%	16	6.2%	9	5.5%	9	6.5%	4	9.1%	4	5.6%	5	7.9%	1	1.6%	5	7.5%	19	6.2%
Discipline-specific knowledge	5	10.0%	37	14.3%	21	12.9%	20	14.5%	7	15.9%	8	11.3%	8	12.7%	8	12.7%	11	16.4%	42	13.6%

Table continues on page 78

Table continued from page 77

Q2. Which of the following campus-wide objectives has your institution identified specifically for sophomores? (Select all that apply.)

Survey question/ responses	Institutional type				Institution control				Number of undergraduates enrolled										Total	
	Two-year		Four-year		Public		Private		Fewer than 1,000		1,001-2,500		2,501-5,000		5,001-10,000		More than 10,000			
	Freq.	%	Freq.	%	Freq.	%	Freq.	%	Freq.	%	Freq.	%	Freq.	%	Freq.	%	Freq.	%	Freq.	%
Graduate or professional school preparation (e.g., premed, pre law)	0	0.0%	43	16.7%	24	14.7%	19	13.8%	4	9.1%	7	9.9%	12	19.0%	7	11.1%	13	19.4%	43	14.0%
Health and wellness	3	6.0%	46	17.8%	24	14.7%	23	16.7%	8	18.2%	9	12.7%	8	12.7%	10	15.9%	14	20.9%	49	15.9%
Information literacy	5	10.0%	21	8.1%	14	8.6%	9	6.5%	6	13.6%	4	5.6%	7	11.1%	4	6.3%	5	7.5%	26	8.4%
Integrative and applied learning	1	2.0%	33	12.8%	15	9.2%	17	12.3%	6	13.6%	6	8.5%	8	12.7%	6	9.5%	8	11.9%	34	11.0%
Intercultural competence, diversity skills, or engaging with different perspectives	8	16.0%	43	16.7%	24	14.7%	27	19.6%	7	15.9%	9	12.7%	11	17.5%	12	19.0%	12	17.9%	51	16.6%
Introduction to a major, discipline, or career path	8	16.0%	82	31.8%	48	29.4%	39	28.3%	12	27.3%	20	28.2%	15	23.8%	17	27.0%	26	38.8%	90	29.2%
Introduction to college-level academic expectations	2	4.0%	28	10.9%	17	10.4%	10	7.2%	5	11.4%	5	7.0%	5	7.9%	7	11.1%	8	11.9%	30	9.7%
Introduction to the liberal arts	1	2.0%	16	6.2%	9	5.5%	8	5.8%	2	4.5%	3	4.2%	4	6.3%	6	9.5%	2	3.0%	17	5.5%
Knowledge of institution or campus resources and services	4	8.0%	64	24.8%	41	25.2%	25	18.1%	7	15.9%	11	15.5%	9	14.3%	16	25.4%	25	37.3%	68	22.1%
Major exploration	2	4.0%	83	32.2%	44	27.0%	40	29.0%	10	22.7%	20	28.2%	16	25.4%	14	22.2%	25	37.3%	85	27.6%

Table continues on page 79

Table continued from page 78

| | Institutional type | | | | Institution control | | | | Number of undergraduates enrolled | | | | | | | | | | | Total | |
| | Two-year | | Four-year | | Public | | Private | | Fewer than 1,000 | | 1,001-2,500 | | 2,501-5,000 | | 5,001-10,000 | | More than 10,000 | | | |
Survey question/ responses	Freq.	%	Freq.	%	Freq.	%	Freq.	%	Freq.	%	Freq.	%	Freq.	%	Freq.	%	Freq.	%	Freq.	%
Q2. Which of the following campus-wide objectives has your institution identified specifically for sophomores? (Select all that apply.)																				
Oral communication skills	5	10.0%	38	14.7%	17	10.4%	22	15.9%	10	22.7%	9	12.7%	10	15.9%	6	9.5%	8	11.9%	43	14.0%
Persistence, retention, or third-year return rates	9	18.0%	87	33.7%	54	33.1%	40	29.0%	12	27.3%	21	29.6%	19	30.2%	12	19.0%	32	47.8%	96	31.2%
Personal exploration or development	6	12.0%	62	24.0%	36	22.1%	31	22.5%	10	22.7%	16	22.5%	9	14.3%	12	19.0%	21	31.3%	68	22.1%
Project planning, teamwork, or management skills	3	6.0%	21	8.1%	12	7.4%	11	8.0%	3	6.8%	6	8.5%	4	6.3%	4	6.3%	7	10.4%	24	7.8%
Social support networks (e.g., friendships)	8	16.0%	53	20.5%	35	21.5%	24	17.4%	7	15.9%	16	22.5%	10	15.9%	11	17.5%	17	25.4%	61	19.8%
Student-faculty interaction	5	10.0%	78	30.2%	42	25.8%	39	28.3%	13	29.5%	17	23.9%	16	25.4%	17	27.0%	20	29.9%	83	26.9%
Writing skills	4	8.0%	39	15.1%	16	9.8%	23	16.7%	11	25.0%	6	8.5%	10	15.9%	7	11.1%	9	13.4%	43	14.0%
Other	8	16.0%	30	11.6%	23	14.1%	14	10.1%	4	9.1%	8	11.3%	7	11.1%	10	15.9%	9	13.4%	38	12.3%
Our institution has not identified campus-wide objectives specifically for the sophomore year	21	42.0%	77	29.8%	56	34.4%	40	29.0%	16	36.4%	20	28.2%	23	36.5%	23	36.5%	16	23.9%	98	31.8%
Total	50	100.0%	258	100.0%	163	100.0%	138	100.0%	44	100.0%	71	100.0%	63	100.0%	63	100.0%	67	100.0%	308	100.0%

Table continues on page 80

Table continued from page 79

Q3. Which of the following institutional efforts have included a specific focus on sophomores? (Select all that apply)

Survey question/ responses	Institutional type				Institution control				Number of undergraduates enrolled										Total	
	Two-year		Four-year		Public		Private		Fewer than 1,000		1,001-2,500		2,501-5,000		5,001-10,000		More than 10,000			
	Freq.	%	Freq.	%	Freq.	%	Freq.	%	Freq.	%	Freq.	%	Freq.	%	Freq.	%	Freq.	%	Freq.	%
Accreditation (e.g., Action Project or Quality Enhancement Plan focused on sophomore-year students)	1	2.0%	17	6.6%	4	2.5%	12	8.7%	2	4.5%	5	7.0%	7	11.1%	3	4.8%	1	1.5%	18	5.8%
Advising study	11	22.0%	50	19.4%	30	18.4%	28	20.3%	10	22.7%	11	15.5%	13	20.6%	10	15.9%	17	25.4%	61	19.8%
Curricular or gateway course redesign	6	12.0%	41	15.9%	23	14.1%	23	16.7%	5	11.4%	14	19.7%	12	19.0%	6	9.5%	10	14.9%	47	15.3%
Employment or job-placement study	10	20.0%	21	8.1%	16	9.8%	13	9.4%	4	9.1%	6	8.5%	8	12.7%	7	11.1%	6	9.0%	31	10.1%
Graduation study	7	14.0%	13	5.0%	14	8.6%	5	3.6%	5	11.4%	2	2.8%	4	6.3%	3	4.8%	6	9.0%	20	6.5%
Grant-funded project	4	8.0%	21	8.1%	14	8.6%	11	8.0%	4	9.1%	8	11.3%	2	3.2%	4	6.3%	7	10.4%	25	8.1%
Institutional assessment	13	26.0%	60	23.3%	40	24.5%	32	23.2%	9	20.5%	16	22.5%	12	19.0%	19	30.2%	17	25.4%	73	23.7%
Participation in a national survey of sophomore-year students (e.g., Noel-Levitz, Sophomore Experiences Survey)	2	4.0%	26	10.1%	16	9.8%	12	8.7%	3	6.8%	6	8.5%	7	11.1%	5	7.9%	7	10.4%	28	9.1%
Pathways programs or meta-majors	9	18.0%	16	6.2%	20	12.3%	5	3.6%	1	2.3%	5	7.0%	4	6.3%	9	14.3%	6	9.0%	25	8.1%
Program self-study	4	8.0%	17	6.6%	14	8.6%	7	5.1%	3	6.8%	3	4.2%	5	7.9%	4	6.3%	6	9.0%	21	6.8%
Retention study	8	16.0%	95	36.8%	46	28.2%	54	39.1%	14	31.8%	25	35.2%	21	33.3%	19	30.2%	24	35.8%	103	33.4%
Strategic planning	7	14.0%	57	22.1%	32	19.6%	31	22.5%	6	13.6%	20	28.2%	12	19.0%	10	15.9%	16	23.9%	64	20.8%

Table continues on page 81

Table continued from page 80

Survey question/responses	Institutional type				Institution control				Number of undergraduates enrolled										Total	
	Two-year		Four-year		Public		Private		Fewer than 1,000		1,001-2,500		2,501-5,000		5,001-10,000		More than 10,000			
	Freq.	%	Freq.	%	Freq.	%	Freq.	%	Freq.	%	Freq.	%	Freq.	%	Freq.	%	Freq.	%	Freq.	%
Q3. Which of the following institutional efforts have included a specific focus on sophomores? (Select all that apply)																				
Student services programming	7	14.0%	77	29.8%	41	25.2%	40	29.0%	11	25.0%	19	26.8%	13	20.6%	19	30.2%	22	32.8%	84	27.3%
Other, please specify	5	10.0%	17	6.6%	14	8.6%	8	5.8%	2	4.5%	6	8.5%	4	6.3%	4	6.3%	6	9.0%	22	7.1%
Our institution has not engaged in any efforts with a specific focus on the sophomore year	19	38.0%	87	33.7%	59	36.2%	44	31.9%	19	43.2%	19	26.8%	26	41.3%	22	34.9%	20	29.9%	106	34.4%
Total	50	100.0%	258	100.0%	163	100.0%	138	100.0%	44	100.0%	71	100.0%	63	100.0%	63	100.0%	67	100.0%	308	100.0%
Q4. How long have your institutional efforts included a specific focus on sophomores?																				
1 year or less	3	9.7%	38	22.4%	22	21.4%	18	19.1%	5	20.0%	10	19.2%	9	24.3%	9	22.0%	8	17.4%	41	20.4%
2-5 years	17	54.8%	80	47.1%	48	46.6%	49	52.1%	13	52.0%	27	51.9%	19	51.4%	19	46.3%	19	41.3%	97	48.3%
6-10 years	2	6.5%	30	17.6%	20	19.4%	11	11.7%	3	12.0%	6	11.5%	3	8.1%	7	17.1%	13	28.3%	32	15.9%
11-15 years	3	9.7%	15	8.8%	6	5.8%	11	11.7%	2	8.0%	5	9.6%	5	13.5%	2	4.9%	4	8.7%	18	9.0%
16-20 years	0	0.0%	3	1.8%	1	1.0%	1	1.1%	1	4.0%	1	1.9%	0	0.0%	0	0.0%	1	2.2%	3	1.5%
More than 20 years	6	19.4%	4	2.4%	6	5.8%	4	4.3%	1	4.0%	3	5.8%	1	2.7%	4	9.8%	1	2.2%	10	5.0%
Total	31	100.0%	170	100.0%	103	100.0%	94	100.0%	25	100.0%	52	100.0%	37	100.0%	41	100.0%	46	100.0%	201	100.0%
Q5. Does your institution currently offer any initiatives specifically or intentionally geared toward sophomore students?																				
Yes	17	34.0%	140	54.5%	79	48.8%	75	54.3%	17	38.6%	39	54.9%	28	44.4%	32	50.8%	41	62.1%	157	51.1%
No	30	60.0%	105	40.9%	71	43.8%	60	43.5%	26	59.1%	31	43.7%	33	52.4%	24	38.1%	21	31.8%	135	44.0%
I don't know.	3	6.0%	12	4.7%	12	7.4%	3	2.2%	1	2.3%	1	1.4%	2	3.2%	7	11.1%	4	6.1%	15	4.9%
Total	50	100.0%	257	100.0%	162	100.0%	138	100.0%	44	100.0%	71	100.0%	63	100.0%	63	100.0%	66	100.0%	307	100.0%

Table continues on page 82

Table continued from page 81

Q6. In which of the following areas does your institution currently have initiatives specifically or intentionally geared toward sophomore students? (Select all that apply)

Survey question/responses	Institutional type				Institution control				Number of undergraduates enrolled										Total	
	Two-year		Four-year		Public		Private		Fewer than 1,000		1,001-2,500		2,501-5,000		5,001-10,000		More than 10,000			
	Freq.	%	Freq.	%	Freq.	%	Freq.	%	Freq.	%	Freq.	%	Freq.	%	Freq.	%	Freq.	%	Freq.	%
Academic advising	13	76.5%	78	56.1%	48	60.8%	40	54.1%	10	58.8%	25	64.1%	16	57.1%	17	54.8%	23	56.1%	91	58.3%
Academic coaching or mentoring	8	47.1%	53	38.1%	32	40.5%	26	35.1%	6	35.3%	15	38.5%	12	42.9%	10	32.3%	18	43.9%	61	39.1%
Back-to-school events	1	5.9%	41	29.5%	18	22.8%	23	31.1%	3	17.6%	13	33.3%	2	7.1%	10	32.3%	14	34.1%	42	26.9%
Campus-based event (e.g., common reading experiences, dinners, fairs)	2	11.8%	49	35.3%	20	25.3%	30	40.5%	4	23.5%	13	33.3%	6	21.4%	13	41.9%	15	36.6%	51	32.7%
Career exploration	8	47.1%	86	61.9%	49	62.0%	44	59.5%	12	70.6%	23	59.0%	14	50.0%	19	61.3%	26	63.4%	94	60.3%
Career planning	12	70.6%	70	50.4%	41	51.9%	39	52.7%	12	70.6%	22	56.4%	16	57.1%	14	45.2%	18	43.9%	82	52.6%
Communication or publications (e.g., social media, newsletter, emails, brochures)	2	11.8%	39	28.1%	21	26.6%	18	24.3%	2	11.8%	8	20.5%	6	21.4%	10	32.3%	15	36.6%	41	26.3%
Course-specific support for classes with high D/F/W rates	2	11.8%	25	18.0%	18	22.8%	9	12.2%	2	11.8%	3	7.7%	7	25.0%	6	19.4%	9	22.0%	27	17.3%
Credit-bearing course (e.g., sophomore seminar)	0	0.0%	19	13.7%	9	11.4%	10	13.5%	2	11.8%	8	20.5%	1	3.6%	1	3.2%	7	17.1%	19	12.2%
Cultural enrichment activities	3	17.6%	15	10.8%	8	10.1%	9	12.2%	4	23.5%	5	12.8%	4	14.3%	2	6.5%	3	7.3%	18	11.5%
Early alert systems	7	41.2%	41	29.5%	22	27.8%	25	33.8%	6	35.3%	16	41.0%	10	35.7%	7	22.6%	9	22.0%	48	30.8%
Faculty or staff mentors	4	23.5%	31	22.3%	17	21.5%	17	23.0%	2	11.8%	8	20.5%	12	42.9%	2	6.5%	11	26.8%	35	22.4%

Table continues on page 83

Table continued from page 82

Survey question/responses	Two-year Freq.	Two-year %	Four-year Freq.	Four-year %	Public Freq.	Public %	Private Freq.	Private %	Fewer than 1,000 Freq.	Fewer than 1,000 %	1,001-2,500 Freq.	1,001-2,500 %	2,501-5,000 Freq.	2,501-5,000 %	5,001-10,000 Freq.	5,001-10,000 %	More than 10,000 Freq.	More than 10,000 %	Total Freq.	Total %
Financial aid	5	29.4%	18	12.9%	13	16.5%	8	10.8%	3	17.6%	4	10.3%	6	21.4%	4	12.9%	6	14.6%	23	14.7%
Internships or co-ops	6	35.3%	26	18.7%	17	21.5%	14	18.9%	4	23.5%	9	23.1%	7	25.0%	5	16.1%	7	17.1%	32	20.5%
Leadership development	6	35.3%	48	34.5%	23	29.1%	30	40.5%	6	35.3%	14	35.9%	12	42.9%	8	25.8%	14	34.1%	54	34.6%
Learning communities	2	11.8%	18	12.9%	8	10.1%	11	14.9%	2	11.8%	3	7.7%	5	17.9%	4	12.9%	6	14.6%	20	12.8%
Major exploration and selection	2	11.8%	52	37.4%	25	31.6%	29	39.2%	6	35.3%	13	33.3%	10	35.7%	10	32.3%	15	36.6%	54	34.6%
Off-campus event (e.g., retreat, outdoor adventure)	1	5.9%	19	13.7%	13	16.5%	7	9.5%	2	11.8%	5	12.8%	1	3.6%	3	9.7%	9	22.0%	20	12.8%
Opportunities to co-teach	0	0.0%	9	6.5%	5	6.3%	4	5.4%	1	5.9%	2	5.1%	0	0.0%	2	6.5%	4	9.8%	9	5.8%
Peer mentoring by sophomores	3	17.6%	39	28.1%	19	24.1%	22	29.7%	3	17.6%	9	23.1%	8	28.6%	9	29.0%	13	31.7%	42	26.9%
Peer mentors for sophomores	2	11.8%	26	18.7%	17	21.5%	11	14.9%	0	0.0%	4	10.3%	7	25.0%	6	19.4%	11	26.8%	28	17.9%
Practica or other supervised practice experiences	1	5.9%	8	5.8%	3	3.8%	6	8.1%	1	5.9%	2	5.1%	3	10.7%	2	6.5%	1	2.4%	9	5.8%
Residence life - sophomore live on-campus requirement	0	0.0%	33	23.7%	7	8.9%	26	35.1%	3	17.6%	11	28.2%	7	25.0%	7	22.6%	5	12.2%	33	21.2%
Residence life - sophomore-specific living learning community	0	0.0%	20	14.4%	9	11.4%	11	14.9%	1	5.9%	3	7.7%	3	10.7%	6	19.4%	7	17.1%	20	12.8%

Table continues on page 84

Table continued from page 83

Survey question/ responses	Institutional type				Institution control				Number of undergraduates enrolled										Total	
	Two-year		Four-year		Public		Private		Fewer than 1,000		1,001-2,500		2,501-5,000		5,001-10,000		More than 10,000			
	Freq.	%	Freq.	%	Freq.	%	Freq.	%	Freq.	%	Freq.	%	Freq.	%	Freq.	%	Freq.	%	Freq.	%
Q6. In which of the following areas does your institution currently have initiatives specifically or intentionally geared toward sophomore students? (Select all that apply)																				
Residence life-sophomore-specific residential curriculum	0	0.0%	18	12.9%	11	13.9%	7	9.5%	0	0.0%	5	12.8%	2	7.1%	2	6.5%	9	22.0%	18	11.5%
Service-learning or community service	3	17.6%	37	26.6%	17	21.5%	22	29.7%	5	29.4%	8	20.5%	9	32.1%	8	25.8%	10	24.4%	40	25.6%
Student government	1	5.9%	26	18.7%	9	11.4%	17	23.0%	2	11.8%	6	15.4%	5	17.9%	9	29.0%	5	12.2%	27	17.3%
Study abroad	2	11.8%	27	19.4%	12	15.2%	17	23.0%	3	17.6%	9	23.1%	5	17.9%	2	6.5%	10	24.4%	29	18.6%
Undergraduate research	2	11.8%	29	20.9%	16	20.3%	15	20.3%	4	23.5%	6	15.4%	4	14.3%	6	19.4%	11	26.8%	31	19.9%
Other	2	11.8%	19	13.7%	12	15.2%	9	12.2%	5	29.4%	5	12.8%	1	3.6%	5	16.1%	5	12.2%	21	13.5%
Total	17	100.0%	139	100.0%	79	100.0%	74	100.0%	17	100.0%	39	100.0%	28	100.0%	31	100.0%	41	100.0%	156	100.0%
Q7. On your campus, how coordinated are sophomore-year initiatives? (Select the most appropriate answer)																				
1 - Totally decentralized, no coordination between any departments or units in sophomore-year initiatives	2	11.8%	17	12.2%	11	13.9%	7	9.5%	3	17.6%	4	10.3%	3	10.7%	2	6.5%	7	17.1%	19	12.2%
2	3	17.6%	34	24.5%	21	26.6%	16	21.6%	2	11.8%	8	20.5%	5	17.9%	9	29.0%	13	31.7%	37	23.7%
3	8	47.1%	51	36.7%	31	39.2%	28	37.8%	5	29.4%	17	43.6%	11	39.3%	15	48.4%	11	26.8%	59	37.8%
4	2	11.8%	23	16.5%	8	10.1%	16	21.6%	5	29.4%	5	12.8%	4	14.3%	4	12.9%	7	17.1%	25	16.0%
5 - Totally centralized, all sophomore-year initiatives are coordinated by a single director or office	2	11.8%	12	8.6%	7	8.9%	6	8.1%	1	5.9%	5	12.8%	5	17.9%	1	3.2%	2	4.9%	14	9.0%

Table continues on page 85

Table continued from page 84

Survey question/ responses	Institutional type				Institution control				Number of undergraduates enrolled										Total	
	Two-year		Four-year		Public		Private		Fewer than 1,000		1,001-2,500		2,501-5,000		5,001-10,000		More than 10,000			
	Freq.	%	Freq.	%	Freq.	%	Freq.	%	Freq.	%	Freq.	%	Freq.	%	Freq.	%	Freq.	%	Freq.	%
Q7. On your campus, how coordinated are sophomore-year initiatives? (Select the most appropriate answer)																				
Don't know	0	0.0%	2	1.4%	1	1.3%	1	1.4%	1	5.9%	0	0.0%	0	0.0%	0	0.0%	1	2.4%	2	1.3%
Total	17	100.0%	139	100.0%	79	100.0%	74	100.0%	17	100.0%	39	100.0%	28	100.0%	31	100.0%	41	100.0%	156	100.0%
Q8. Which campus units participate in the coordination of their sophomore-year initiatives? (Select all that apply)																				
Academic advising	12	92.3%	73	67.6%	48	80.0%	36	60.0%	9	75.0%	18	60.0%	15	75.0%	18	64.3%	25	80.6%	85	70.2%
Academic affairs central office	5	38.5%	53	49.1%	29	48.3%	29	48.3%	6	50.0%	16	53.3%	11	55.0%	10	35.7%	15	48.4%	58	47.9%
Academic department(s), please specify	6	46.2%	20	18.5%	12	20.0%	13	21.7%	3	25.0%	7	23.3%	7	35.0%	4	14.3%	5	16.1%	26	21.5%
Career services	8	61.5%	67	62.0%	36	60.0%	38	63.3%	9	75.0%	18	60.0%	13	65.0%	16	57.1%	19	61.3%	75	62.0%
Center for teaching excellence	1	7.7%	2	1.9%	2	3.3%	1	1.7%	1	8.3%	1	3.3%	0	0.0%	0	0.0%	1	3.2%	3	2.5%
Enrollment management central office	4	30.8%	20	18.5%	16	26.7%	8	13.3%	1	8.3%	4	13.3%	6	30.0%	5	17.9%	8	25.8%	24	19.8%
Residence life or housing	1	7.7%	48	44.4%	21	35.0%	28	46.7%	4	33.3%	12	40.0%	7	35.0%	14	50.0%	12	38.7%	49	40.5%
Student activities and leadership	9	69.2%	53	49.1%	30	50.0%	31	51.7%	6	50.0%	14	46.7%	13	65.0%	14	50.0%	15	48.4%	62	51.2%
Student affairs central office	6	46.2%	46	42.6%	27	45.0%	25	41.7%	6	50.0%	13	43.3%	11	55.0%	12	42.9%	10	32.3%	52	43.0%
Student success center	5	38.5%	48	44.4%	29	48.3%	24	40.0%	3	25.0%	14	46.7%	9	45.0%	9	32.1%	18	58.1%	53	43.8%
Other, please specify	2	15.4%	23	21.3%	15	25.0%	10	16.7%	1	8.3%	5	16.7%	4	20.0%	7	25.0%	8	25.8%	25	20.7%
Total	13	100.0%	108	100.0%	60	100.0%	60	100.0%	12	100.0%	30	100.0%	20	100.0%	28	100.0%	31	100.0%	121	100.0%

Table continues on page 86

Table continued from page 85

Survey question/responses	Institutional type				Institution control				Number of undergraduates enrolled										Total	
	Two-year		Four-year		Public		Private		Fewer than 1,000		1,001-2,500		2,501-5,000		5,001-10,000		More than 10,000			
	Freq.	%	Freq	%	Freq.	%	Freq.	%	Freq.	%	Freq.	%	Freq.	%	Freq.	%	Freq.	%	Freq.	%
Q9. Is there currently an individual in charge of sophomore student programs or initiatives?																				
Yes	5	29.4%	56	40.3%	30	38.0%	29	39.2%	4	23.5%	19	48.7%	10	35.7%	10	32.3%	18	43.9%	61	39.1%
No	12	70.6%	83	59.7%	49	62.0%	45	60.8%	13	76.5%	20	51.3%	18	64.3%	21	67.7%	23	56.1%	95	60.9%
Total	17	100.0%	139	100.0%	79	100.0%	74	100.0%	17	100.0%	39	100.0%	28	100.0%	31	100.0%	41	100.0%	156	100.0%
Q11. Is this position dedicated to sophomore programs and initiatives on a full-time basis (approximately 40 hours per week)?																				
Yes	1	20.0%	14	25.0%	7	23.3%	6	20.7%	1	25.0%	5	26.3%	1	10.0%	2	20.0%	6	33.3%	15	24.6%
No	4	80.0%	41	73.2%	22	73.3%	23	79.3%	3	75.0%	14	73.7%	9	90.0%	8	80.0%	11	61.1%	45	73.8%
I don't know	0	0.0%	1	1.8%	1	3.3%	0	0.0%	0	0.0%	0	0.0%	0	0.0%	0	0.0%	1	5.6%	1	1.6%
Total	5	100.0%	56	100.0%	30	100.0%	29	100.0%	4	100.0%	19	100.0%	10	100.0%	10	100.0%	18	100.0%	61	100.0%
Q12. Does this person have another position on campus?																				
Yes	2	50.0%	32	76.2%	18	78.3%	16	69.6%	2	66.7%	10	71.4%	7	77.8%	6	75.0%	9	75.0%	34	73.9%
No	2	50.0%	10	23.8%	5	21.7%	7	30.4%	1	33.3%	4	28.6%	2	22.2%	2	25.0%	3	25.0%	12	26.1%
Total	4	100.0%	42	100.0%	23	100.0%	23	100.0%	3	100.0%	14	100.0%	9	100.0%	8	100.0%	12	100.0%	46	100.0%
Q13. The other campus role of the director, coordinator, or dean of the sophomore initiative is a/an: (Select all that apply)																				
Academic affairs administrator	0	0.0%	10	31.3%	7	38.9%	3	18.8%	0	0.0%	2	20.0%	3	42.9%	0	0.0%	5	55.6%	10	29.4%
Adjunct or part-time faculty member	1	50.0%	1	3.1%	1	5.6%	1	6.3%	0	0.0%	1	10.0%	0	0.0%	1	16.7%	0	0.0%	2	5.9%
Full-time or tenure-track faculty member	6	300.0%	1	3.1%	2	11.1%	5	31.3%	1	50.0%	3	30.0%	0	0.0%	1	16.7%	2	22.2%	7	20.6%
Student affairs administrator	0	0.0%	11	34.4%	6	33.3%	5	31.3%	1	50.0%	4	40.0%	1	14.3%	3	50.0%	2	22.2%	11	32.4%

Table continues on page 87

Table continued from page 86

Survey question/responses	Two-year Freq	Two-year %	Four-year Freq	Four-year %	Public Freq.	Public %	Private Freq.	Private %	Fewer than 1,000 Freq.	Fewer than 1,000 %	1,001-2,500 Freq.	1,001-2,500 %	2,501-5,000 Freq.	2,501-5,000 %	5,001-10,000 Freq.	5,001-10,000 %	More than 10,000 Freq.	More than 10,000 %	Total Freq.	Total %
	Institutional type				**Institution control**				**Number of undergraduates enrolled**										**Total**	
Q13. The other campus role of the director, coordinator, or dean of the sophomore initiative is a/an: (Select all that apply)																				
Other, please specify	0	0.0%	11	34.4%	5	27.8%	6	37.5%	0	0.0%	4	40.0%	4	57.1%	2	33.3%	1	11.1%	11	32.4%
Total	2	100.0%	32	100.0%	18	100.0%	16	100.0%	2	100.0%	10	100.0%	7	100.0%	6	100.0%	9	100.0%	34	100.0%
Q14. Which of the following initiatives reaches the highest proportion of sophomore students at your institution? (Select only one)																				
Academic advising	9	52.9%	53	38.4%	34	43.0%	26	35.6%	7	41.2%	15	38.5%	8	28.6%	13	43.3%	19	46.3%	62	40.0%
Academic coaching or mentoring	2	11.8%	7	5.1%	7	8.9%	2	2.7%	1	5.9%	3	7.7%	1	3.6%	0	0.0%	4	9.8%	9	5.8%
Back-to-school events	0	0.0%	5	3.6%	1	1.3%	4	5.5%	1	5.9%	3	7.7%	0	0.0%	1	3.3%	0	0.0%	5	3.2%
Campus-based event (e.g., common reading experiences, dinners, fairs)	0	0.0%	6	4.3%	2	2.5%	4	5.5%	1	5.9%	0	0.0%	3	10.7%	2	6.7%	0	0.0%	6	3.9%
Career exploration	1	5.9%	9	6.5%	3	3.8%	7	9.6%	2	11.8%	4	10.3%	1	3.6%	1	3.3%	2	4.9%	10	6.5%
Career planning	2	11.8%	3	2.2%	3	3.8%	1	1.4%	1	5.9%	1	2.6%	2	7.1%	0	0.0%	1	2.4%	5	3.2%
Communication or publications (e.g., social media, newsletter, emails, brochures)	0	0.0%	6	4.3%	5	6.3%	1	1.4%	0	0.0%	1	2.6%	0	0.0%	2	6.7%	3	7.3%	6	3.9%
Course-specific support for classes with high D/F/W rates	0	0.0%	0	0.0%	0	0.0%	0	0.0%	0	0.0%	0	0.0%	0	0.0%	0	0.0%	0	0.0%	0	0.0%
Credit-bearing course (e.g., sophomore seminar)	0	0.0%	5	3.6%	2	2.5%	3	4.1%	0	0.0%	1	2.6%	0	0.0%	2	6.7%	2	4.9%	5	3.2%
Cultural enrichment activities	0	0.0%	0	0.0%	0	0.0%	0	0.0%	0	0.0%	0	0.0%	0	0.0%	0	0.0%	0	0.0%	0	0.0%

Table continues on page 88

Table continued from page 87

Q14. Which of the following initiatives reaches the highest proportion of sophomore students at your institution? (Select only one)

Survey question/ responses	Institutional type				Institution control				Number of undergraduates enrolled										Total	
	Two-year		Four-year		Public		Private		Fewer than 1,000		1,001-2,500		2,501-5,000		5,001-10,000		More than 10,000			
	Freq.	%	Freq.	%	Freq.	%	Freq.	%	Freq.	%	Freq.	%	Freq.	%	Freq.	%	Freq.	%	Freq.	%
Early alert systems	0	0.0%	6	4.3%	5	6.3%	1	1.4%	0	0.0%	1	2.6%	3	10.7%	1	3.3%	1	2.4%	6	3.9%
Faculty or staff mentors	0	0.0%	1	0.7%	0	0.0%	1	1.4%	0	0.0%	1	2.6%	0	0.0%	0	0.0%	0	0.0%	1	0.6%
Financial aid	0	0.0%	1	0.7%	1	1.3%	0	0.0%	0	0.0%	1	2.6%	0	0.0%	0	0.0%	0	0.0%	1	0.6%
Internships or co-ops	0	0.0%	1	0.7%	0	0.0%	1	1.4%	0	0.0%	0	0.0%	0	0.0%	1	3.3%	0	0.0%	1	0.6%
Leadership development	1	5.9%	4	2.9%	2	2.5%	3	4.1%	1	5.9%	1	2.6%	1	3.6%	1	3.3%	1	2.4%	5	3.2%
Learning communities	0	0.0%	1	0.7%	1	1.3%	0	0.0%	0	0.0%	0	0.0%	1	3.6%	0	0.0%	0	0.0%	1	0.6%
Major exploration and selection	0	0.0%	3	2.2%	1	1.3%	2	2.7%	0	0.0%	2	5.1%	0	0.0%	1	3.3%	0	0.0%	3	1.9%
Off-campus event (e.g., retreat, outdoor adventure)	0	0.0%	1	0.7%	1	1.3%	0	0.0%	0	0.0%	0	0.0%	0	0.0%	0	0.0%	1	2.4%	1	0.6%
Opportunities to co-teach or assist in teaching a class	0	0.0%	0	0.0%	0	0.0%	0	0.0%	0	0.0%	0	0.0%	0	0.0%	0	0.0%	0	0.0%	0	0.0%
Peer mentoring by sophomores	0	0.0%	1	0.7%	1	1.3%	0	0.0%	0	0.0%	0	0.0%	1	3.6%	0	0.0%	0	0.0%	1	0.6%
Peer mentors for sophomores	1	5.9%	1	0.7%	1	1.3%	1	1.4%	0	0.0%	0	0.0%	1	3.6%	1	3.3%	0	0.0%	2	1.3%
Practica or other supervised practice experiences	0	0.0%	0	0.0%	0	0.0%	0	0.0%	0	0.0%	0	0.0%	0	0.0%	0	0.0%	0	0.0%	0	0.0%
Residence life - sophomore live on-campus requirement	0	0.0%	10	7.2%	2	2.5%	8	11.0%	0	0.0%	2	5.1%	3	10.7%	2	6.7%	3	7.3%	10	6.5%

Table continues on page 89

Table continued from page 88

Survey question/responses	Institutional type				Institution control				Number of undergraduates enrolled										Total	
	Two-year		Four-year		Public		Private		Fewer than 1,000		1,001-2,500		2,501-5,000		5,001-10,000		More than 10,000			
	Freq.	%	Freq	%	Freq.	%	Freq.	%	Freq.	%	Freq.	%	Freq.	%	Freq.	%	Freq.	%	Freq.	%
Q14. Which of the following initiatives reaches the highest proportion of sophomore students at your institution? (Select only one)																				
Residence life - sophomore-specific living learning community	0	0.0%	1	0.7%	0	0.0%	1	1.4%	0	0.0%	0	0.0%	1	3.6%	0	0.0%	0	0.0%	1	0.6%
Residence life- sophomore-specific residential curriculum	0	0.0%	3	2.2%	2	2.5%	1	1.4%	0	0.0%	1	2.6%	0	0.0%	1	3.3%	1	2.4%	3	1.9%
Service-learning or community service	0	0.0%	2	1.4%	1	1.3%	1	1.4%	0	0.0%	1	2.6%	0	0.0%	0	0.0%	1	2.4%	2	1.3%
Student government	0	0.0%	1	0.7%	0	0.0%	1	1.4%	0	0.0%	0	0.0%	0	0.0%	0	0.0%	1	2.4%	1	0.6%
Study abroad	0	0.0%	2	1.4%	0	0.0%	2	2.7%	0	0.0%	1	2.6%	1	3.6%	0	0.0%	0	0.0%	2	1.3%
Undergraduate research	0	0.0%	0	0.0%	0	0.0%	0	0.0%	0	0.0%	0	0.0%	0	0.0%	0	0.0%	0	0.0%	0	0.0%
Other	1	5.9%	5	3.6%	4	5.1%	2	2.7%	3	17.6%	0	0.0%	1	3.6%	1	3.3%	1	2.4%	6	3.9%
Total	17	100.0%	138	100.0%	79	100.0%	73	100.0%	17	100.0%	39	100.0%	28	100.0%	30	100.0%	41	100.0%	155	100.0%
Q15. Which of the following are the primary sophomore-year programs by which the campuswide objectives for sophomores are met? (Please select up to 5)																				
Academic advising	13	81.3%	80	58.4%	52	66.7%	39	54.2%	8	50.0%	23	60.5%	16	57.1%	18	60.0%	28	68.3%	93	60.8%
Academic coaching or mentoring	4	25.0%	25	18.2%	19	24.4%	9	12.5%	3	18.8%	8	21.1%	4	14.3%	3	10.0%	11	26.8%	29	19.0%
Back-to-school events	0	0.0%	14	10.2%	6	7.7%	8	11.1%	1	6.3%	5	13.2%	1	3.6%	4	13.3%	3	7.3%	14	9.2%
Campus-based event (e.g., common reading experiences, dinners, fairs)	1	6.3%	24	17.5%	13	16.7%	12	16.7%	4	25.0%	6	15.8%	3	10.7%	5	16.7%	7	17.1%	25	16.3%
Career exploration	2	12.5%	56	40.9%	25	32.1%	32	44.4%	10	62.5%	14	36.8%	10	35.7%	9	30.0%	15	36.6%	58	37.9%

Table continues on page 90

Table continued from page 89

Q15. Which of the following are the primary sophomore-year programs by which the campuswide objectives for sophomores are met? (Please select up to 5)

Survey question/ responses	Institutional type				Institution control				Number of undergraduates enrolled										Total	
	Two-year		Four-year		Public		Private		Fewer than 1,000		1,001-2,500		2,501-5,000		5,001-10,000		More than 10,000			
	Freq.	%	Freq.	%	Freq.	%	Freq.	%	Freq.	%	Freq.	%	Freq.	%	Freq.	%	Freq.	%	Freq.	%
Career planning	4	25.0%	31	22.6%	17	21.8%	17	23.6%	3	18.8%	10	26.3%	8	28.6%	6	20.0%	8	19.5%	35	22.9%
Communication or publications (e.g., social media, newsletter, emails, brochures)	1	6.3%	19	13.9%	13	16.7%	7	9.7%	0	0.0%	6	15.8%	0	0.0%	5	16.7%	9	22.0%	20	13.1%
Course-specific support for classes with high D/F/W rates	0	0.0%	8	5.8%	5	6.4%	2	2.8%	0	0.0%	1	2.6%	1	3.6%	2	6.7%	4	9.8%	8	5.2%
Credit-bearing course (e.g., sophomore seminar)	0	0.0%	19	13.9%	9	11.5%	9	12.5%	2	12.5%	7	18.4%	0	0.0%	2	6.7%	8	19.5%	19	12.4%
Cultural enrichment activities	2	12.5%	2	1.5%	3	3.8%	0	0.0%	1	6.3%	1	2.6%	1	3.6%	0	0.0%	1	2.4%	4	2.6%
Early alert systems	4	25.0%	19	13.9%	15	19.2%	8	11.1%	2	12.5%	4	10.5%	5	17.9%	5	16.7%	7	17.1%	23	15.0%
Faculty or staff mentors	1	6.3%	14	10.2%	8	10.3%	7	9.7%	2	12.5%	3	7.9%	2	7.1%	3	10.0%	5	12.2%	15	9.8%
Financial aid	2	12.5%	9	6.6%	7	9.0%	3	4.2%	2	12.5%	3	7.9%	4	14.3%	1	3.3%	1	2.4%	11	7.2%
Internships or co-ops	1	6.3%	5	3.6%	3	3.8%	3	4.2%	0	0.0%	1	2.6%	2	7.1%	2	6.7%	1	2.4%	6	3.9%
Leadership development	3	18.8%	26	19.0%	14	17.9%	15	20.8%	4	25.0%	6	15.8%	8	28.6%	5	16.7%	6	14.6%	29	19.0%
Learning communities	0	0.0%	4	2.9%	2	2.6%	2	2.8%	1	6.3%	1	2.6%	1	3.6%	1	3.3%	0	0.0%	4	2.6%
Major exploration and selection	1	6.3%	33	24.1%	12	15.4%	22	30.6%	4	25.0%	10	26.3%	6	21.4%	5	16.7%	9	22.0%	34	22.2%
Off-campus event (e.g., retreat, outdoor adventure)	0	0.0%	7	5.1%	3	3.8%	4	5.6%	1	6.3%	2	5.3%	0	0.0%	2	6.7%	2	4.9%	7	4.6%

Table continues on page 91

Table continued from page 90

Q15. Which of the following are the primary sophomore-year programs by which the campuswide objectives for sophomores are met? (Please select up to 5)

Survey question/ responses	Institutional type				Institution control				Number of undergraduates enrolled										Total	
	Two-year		Four-year		Public		Private		Fewer than 1,000		1,001-2,500		2,501-5,000		5,001-10,000		More than 10,000			
	Freq.	%	Freq.	%	Freq.	%	Freq.	%	Freq.	%	Freq.	%	Freq.	%	Freq.	%	Freq.	%	Freq.	%
Opportunities to co-teach or assist in teaching a class	0	0.0%	3	2.2%	1	1.3%	2	2.8%	0	0.0%	1	2.6%	0	0.0%	1	3.3%	1	2.4%	3	2.0%
Peer mentoring by sophomores	1	6.3%	17	12.4%	7	9.0%	11	15.3%	1	6.3%	5	13.2%	3	10.7%	5	16.7%	4	9.8%	18	11.8%
Peer mentors for sophomores	1	6.3%	8	5.8%	6	7.7%	3	4.2%	0	0.0%	1	2.6%	1	3.6%	2	6.7%	5	12.2%	9	5.9%
Practica or other supervised practice experiences	2	12.5%	0	0.0%	2	2.6%	0	0.0%	0	0.0%	0	0.0%	1	3.6%	1	3.3%	0	0.0%	2	1.3%
Residence life - sophomore live on-campus requirement	0	0.0%	20	14.6%	4	5.1%	16	22.2%	2	12.5%	6	15.8%	5	17.9%	4	13.3%	3	7.3%	20	13.1%
Residence life - sophomore-specific living learning community	0	0.0%	11	8.0%	5	6.4%	6	8.3%	0	0.0%	2	5.3%	1	3.6%	3	10.0%	5	12.2%	11	7.2%
Residence life- sophomore-specific residential curriculum	0	0.0%	11	8.0%	7	9.0%	4	5.6%	0	0.0%	3	7.9%	1	3.6%	3	10.0%	4	9.8%	11	7.2%
Service-learning or community service	2	12.5%	15	10.9%	8	10.3%	9	12.5%	2	12.5%	4	10.5%	6	21.4%	3	10.0%	2	4.9%	17	11.1%
Student government	0	0.0%	3	2.2%	0	0.0%	2	2.8%	0	0.0%	0	0.0%	2	7.1%	1	3.3%	0	0.0%	3	2.0%
Study abroad	0	0.0%	12	8.8%	2	2.6%	10	13.9%	1	6.3%	2	5.3%	4	14.3%	3	10.0%	2	4.9%	12	7.8%
Undergraduate research	2	12.5%	7	5.1%	7	9.0%	2	2.8%	0	0.0%	1	2.6%	1	3.6%	1	3.3%	6	14.6%	9	5.9%

Table continues on page 92

Table continued from page 91

Survey question/ responses	Institutional type				Institution control				Number of undergraduates enrolled										Total	
	Two-year		Four-year		Public		Private		Fewer than 1,000		1,001-2,500		2,501-5,000		5,001-10,000		More than 10,000			
	Freq.	%	Freq.	%	Freq.	%	Freq.	%	Freq.	%	Freq.	%	Freq.	%	Freq.	%	Freq.	%	Freq.	%
Q15. Which of the following are the primary sophomore-year programs by which the campuswide objectives for sophomores are met? (Please select up to 5)																				
Other	2	12.5%	17	12.4%	13	16.7%	6	8.3%	3	18.8%	2	5.3%	2	7.1%	5	16.7%	7	17.1%	19	12.4%
Total	16	100.0%	137	100.0%	78	100.0%	72	100.0%	16	100.0%	38	100.0%	28	100.0%	30	100.0%	41	100.0%	153	100.0%
Q16. What is the approximate percentage of sophomore students this initiative reaches on your campus? (Indicated by answer to Q14)																				
10% or less	1	12.5%	12	14.3%	10	22.2%	3	6.5%	0	0.0%	0	0.0%	3	15.0%	2	11.8%	8	36.4%	13	14.1%
11-20%	0	0.0%	5	6.0%	4	8.9%	1	2.2%	0	0.0%	2	8.3%	1	5.0%	1	5.9%	1	4.5%	5	5.4%
21-30%	3	37.5%	14	16.7%	7	15.6%	10	21.7%	1	11.1%	4	16.7%	6	30.0%	3	17.6%	3	13.6%	17	18.5%
31-40%	1	12.5%	9	10.7%	4	8.9%	6	13.0%	3	33.3%	2	8.3%	2	10.0%	0	0.0%	3	13.6%	10	10.9%
41-50%	1	12.5%	6	7.1%	5	11.1%	2	4.3%	1	11.1%	1	4.2%	1	5.0%	2	11.8%	2	9.1%	7	7.6%
51-60%	0	0.0%	5	6.0%	1	2.2%	3	6.5%	2	22.2%	1	4.2%	0	0.0%	1	5.9%	1	4.5%	5	5.4%
61-70%	1	12.5%	5	6.0%	5	11.1%	1	2.2%	0	0.0%	2	8.3%	1	5.0%	2	11.8%	1	4.5%	6	6.5%
71-80%	0	0.0%	4	4.8%	0	0.0%	4	8.7%	0	0.0%	2	8.3%	0	0.0%	2	11.8%	0	0.0%	4	4.3%
81-90%	1	12.5%	7	8.3%	4	8.9%	4	8.7%	0	0.0%	3	12.5%	2	10.0%	1	5.9%	2	9.1%	8	8.7%
91-100%	0	0.0%	17	20.2%	5	11.1%	12	26.1%	2	22.2%	7	29.2%	4	20.0%	3	17.6%	1	4.5%	17	18.5%
Total	8	100.0%	84	100.0%	45	100.0%	46	100.0%	9	100.0%	24	100.0%	20	100.0%	17	100.0%	22	100.0%	92	100.0%
Q17. What proportion of your sophomore students are required to participate in this initiative?																				
None are required to participate	6	75.0%	54	64.3%	32	71.1%	28	60.9%	6	66.7%	14	58.3%	12	60.0%	12	70.6%	16	72.7%	60	65.2%
Less than 10%	2	25.0%	2	2.4%	4	8.9%	0	0.0%	0	0.0%	0	0.0%	1	5.0%	1	5.9%	2	9.1%	4	4.3%
10-19%	0	0.0%	0	0.0%	0	0.0%	0	0.0%	0	0.0%	0	0.0%	0	0.0%	0	0.0%	0	0.0%	0	0.0%
20-29%	0	0.0%	2	2.4%	2	4.4%	0	0.0%	0	0.0%	1	4.2%	1	5.0%	0	0.0%	0	0.0%	2	2.2%

Table continues on page 93

Table continued from page 92

Survey question/responses	Institutional type				Institution control				Number of undergraduates enrolled										Total	
	Two-year		Four-year		Public		Private		Fewer than 1,000		1,001-2,500		2,501-5,000		5,001-10,000		More than 10,000			
	Freq.	%	Freq	%	Freq.	%	Freq.	%	Freq.	%	Freq.	%	Freq.	%	Freq.	%	Freq.	%	Freq.	%
Q17. What proportion of your sophomore students are required to participate in this initiative?																				
30-39%	0	0.0%	2	2.4%	1	2.2%	1	2.2%	0	0.0%	1	4.2%	0	0.0%	0	0.0%	1	4.5%	2	2.2%
40-49%	0	0.0%	0	0.0%	0	0.0%	0	0.0%	0	0.0%	0	0.0%	0	0.0%	0	0.0%	0	0.0%	0	0.0%
50-59%	0	0.0%	2	2.4%	0	0.0%	2	4.3%	0	0.0%	1	4.2%	0	0.0%	1	5.9%	0	0.0%	2	2.2%
60-69%	0	0.0%	1	1.2%	0	0.0%	1	2.2%	0	0.0%	0	0.0%	1	5.0%	0	0.0%	0	0.0%	1	1.1%
70-79%	0	0.0%	2	2.4%	0	0.0%	2	4.3%	0	0.0%	1	4.2%	0	0.0%	1	5.9%	0	0.0%	2	2.2%
80-89%	0	0.0%	1	1.2%	1	2.2%	0	0.0%	0	0.0%	0	0.0%	0	0.0%	0	0.0%	1	4.5%	1	1.1%
90-99%	0	0.0%	5	6.0%	1	2.2%	4	8.7%	0	0.0%	0	0.0%	1	5.0%	2	11.8%	2	9.1%	5	5.4%
100%- All sophomore students are required to participate	0	0.0%	13	15.5%	4	8.9%	8	17.4%	3	33.3%	6	25.0%	4	20.0%	0	0.0%	0	0.0%	13	14.1%
Total	8	100.0%	84	100.0%	45	100.0%	46	100.0%	9	100.0%	24	100.0%	20	100.0%	17	100.0%	22	100.0%	92	100.0%
Q18. Which of the following groups of sophomore students are required to participate in this initiative? (Select all that apply)																				
Academically underprepared students	0	0.0%	6	37.5%	2	22.2%	4	44.4%	0	-	3	75.0%	2	50.0%	1	25.0%	0	0.0%	6	33.3%
First-generation students	0	0.0%	5	31.3%	1	11.1%	4	44.4%	0	-	2	50.0%	1	25.0%	1	25.0%	1	16.7%	5	27.8%
Honors students	0	0.0%	3	18.8%	0	0.0%	3	33.3%	0	-	1	25.0%	1	25.0%	1	25.0%	0	0.0%	3	16.7%
International students	0	0.0%	3	18.8%	0	0.0%	3	33.3%	0	-	1	25.0%	1	25.0%	1	25.0%	0	0.0%	3	16.7%
Learning community participants	0	0.0%	1	6.3%	0	0.0%	1	11.1%	0	-	0	0.0%	0	0.0%	1	25.0%	0	0.0%	1	5.6%
Preprofessional students (e.g., prelaw, premed)	0	0.0%	1	6.3%	0	0.0%	1	11.1%	0	-	0	0.0%	0	0.0%	1	25.0%	0	0.0%	1	5.6%

Table continues on page 94

Table continued from page 93

Survey question/ responses	Institutional type				Institution control				Number of undergraduates enrolled											Total	
	Two-year		Four-year		Public		Private		Fewer than 1,000		1,001-2,500		2,501-5,000		5,001-10,000		More than 10,000					
	Freq.	%	Freq.	%	Freq.	%	Freq.	%	Freq.	%	Freq.	%	Freq.	%	Freq.	%	Freq.	%	Freq.	%		

Q18. Which of the following groups of sophomore students are required to participate in this initiative? (Select all that apply)

Survey question/ responses	Two-year Freq.	%	Four-year Freq.	%	Public Freq.	%	Private Freq.	%	Fewer than 1,000 Freq.	%	1,001-2,500 Freq.	%	2,501-5,000 Freq.	%	5,001-10,000 Freq.	%	More than 10,000 Freq.	%	Total Freq.	%
Student athletes	0	0.0%	3	18.8%	0	0.0%	3	33.3%	0	-	1	25.0%	1	25.0%	1	25.0%	0	0.0%	3	16.7%
Students enrolled in developmental or remedial courses	0	0.0%	2	12.5%	0	0.0%	2	22.2%	0	-	0	0.0%	1	25.0%	1	25.0%	0	0.0%	2	11.1%
Students on probationary status	0	0.0%	3	18.8%	1	11.1%	2	22.2%	0	-	0	0.0%	2	50.0%	1	25.0%	0	0.0%	3	16.7%
Students residing within a particular residence hall	0	0.0%	2	12.5%	0	0.0%	2	22.2%	0	-	0	0.0%	1	25.0%	1	25.0%	0	0.0%	2	11.1%
Students with fewer credits than necessary for sophomore status	0	0.0%	3	18.8%	1	11.1%	2	22.2%	0	-	0	0.0%	2	50.0%	1	25.0%	0	0.0%	3	16.7%
Students within specific majors	1	50.0%	2	12.5%	2	22.2%	1	11.1%	0	-	0	0.0%	1	25.0%	1	25.0%	1	16.7%	3	16.7%
TRIO participants	0	0.0%	2	12.5%	1	11.1%	1	11.1%	0	-	0	0.0%	1	25.0%	1	25.0%	1	16.7%	2	11.1%
Undeclared students	0	0.0%	3	18.8%	0	0.0%	3	33.3%	0	-	1	25.0%	1	25.0%	1	25.0%	0	0.0%	3	16.7%
Other	1	50.0%	7	43.8%	4	44.4%	4	44.4%	0	-	1	25.0%	1	25.0%	2	50.0%	4	66.7%	8	44.4%
Total	2	100.0%	16	100.0%	9	100.0%	9	100.0%	0	-	4	100.0%	4	100.0%	4	100.0%	6	100.0%	18	100.0%

Q19. Which of the following groups of sophomore students are specifically targeted by this initiative?

Survey question/ responses	Two-year Freq.	%	Four-year Freq.	%	Public Freq.	%	Private Freq.	%	Fewer than 1,000 Freq.	%	1,001-2,500 Freq.	%	2,501-5,000 Freq.	%	5,001-10,000 Freq.	%	More than 10,000 Freq.	%	Total Freq.	%
Academically underprepared students	0	0.0%	16	19.3%	10	22.2%	6	66.7%	0	0.0%	6	25.0%	5	25.0%	2	12.5%	3	13.6%	16	17.6%
First-generation students	1	12.5%	21	25.3%	13	28.9%	9	100.0%	0	0.0%	7	29.2%	5	25.0%	3	18.8%	7	31.8%	22	24.2%
Honors students	0	0.0%	12	14.5%	6	13.3%	6	66.7%	0	0.0%	3	12.5%	3	15.0%	3	18.8%	3	13.6%	12	13.2%

Table continues on page 95

Table continued from page 94

Survey question/ responses	Institutional type				Institution control				Number of undergraduates enrolled										Total	
	Two-year		Four-year		Public		Private		Fewer than 1,000		1,001-2,500		2,501-5,000		5,001-10,000		More than 10,000			
	Freq.	%	Freq.	%	Freq.	%	Freq.	%	Freq.	%	Freq.	%	Freq.	%	Freq.	%	Freq.	%	Freq.	%
Q19. Which of the following groups of sophomore students are specifically targeted by this initiative?																				
International students	1	12.5%	6	7.2%	4	8.9%	3	33.3%	0	0.0%	1	4.2%	4	20.0%	1	6.3%	1	4.5%	7	7.7%
Learning community participants	1	12.5%	2	2.4%	3	6.7%	0	0.0%	0	0.0%	1	4.2%	1	5.0%	0	0.0%	1	4.5%	3	3.3%
Preprofessional students (e.g., prelaw, premed)	0	0.0%	6	7.2%	2	4.4%	4	44.4%	0	0.0%	1	4.2%	2	10.0%	3	18.8%	0	0.0%	6	6.6%
Student athletes	0	0.0%	8	9.6%	4	8.9%	4	44.4%	0	0.0%	4	16.7%	2	10.0%	2	12.5%	0	0.0%	8	8.8%
Students enrolled in developmental or remedial courses	0	0.0%	5	6.0%	3	6.7%	2	22.2%	0	0.0%	1	4.2%	2	10.0%	1	6.3%	1	4.5%	5	5.5%
Students on probationary status	1	12.5%	11	13.3%	9	20.0%	3	33.3%	0	0.0%	3	12.5%	5	25.0%	1	6.3%	3	13.6%	12	13.2%
Students residing within a particular residence hall	0	0.0%	5	6.0%	4	8.9%	1	11.1%	0	0.0%	1	4.2%	1	5.0%	2	12.5%	1	4.5%	5	5.5%
Students with fewer credits than necessary for sophomore status	0	0.0%	5	6.0%	2	4.4%	3	33.3%	0	0.0%	3	12.5%	1	5.0%	1	6.3%	0	0.0%	5	5.5%
Students within specific majors	1	12.5%	6	7.2%	4	8.9%	3	33.3%	0	0.0%	2	8.3%	1	5.0%	2	12.5%	2	9.1%	7	7.7%
TRIO participants	2	25.0%	6	7.2%	7	15.6%	1	11.1%	0	0.0%	4	16.7%	1	5.0%	1	6.3%	2	9.1%	8	8.8%
Undeclared students	0	0.0%	12	14.5%	7	15.6%	5	55.6%	0	0.0%	4	16.7%	4	20.0%	3	18.8%	1	4.5%	12	13.2%
Other	4	50.0%	22	26.5%	12	26.7%	14	155.6%	3	33.3%	5	20.8%	5	25.0%	7	43.8%	6	27.3%	26	28.6%

Table continues on page 96

Table continued from page 95

Survey question/responses	Institutional type				Institution control				Number of undergraduates enrolled										Total	
	Two-year		Four-year		Public		Private		Fewer than 1,000		1,001-2,500		2,501-5,000		5,001-10,000		More than 10,000			
	Freq.	%	Freq.	%	Freq.	%	Freq.	%	Freq.	%	Freq.	%	Freq.	%	Freq.	%	Freq.	%	Freq.	%
Q19. Which of the following groups of sophomore students are specifically targeted by this initiative?																				
No sophomore students are specifically targeted by this initiative	1	12.5%	33	39.8%	14	31.1%	19	211.1%	6	66.7%	9	37.5%	6	30.0%	4	25.0%	9	40.9%	34	37.4%
Total	8	100.0%	83	100.0%	45	100.0%	45	100.0%	9	100.0%	24	100.0%	20	100.0%	16	100.0%	22	100.0%	91	100.0%
Q20. How long has this initiative been in place?																				
2 years or less	2	25.0%	26	31.7%	16	35.6%	12	26.7%	0	0.0%	10	41.7%	10	50.0%	4	25.0%	4	18.2%	28	31.1%
3-5 years	4	50.0%	22	26.8%	12	26.7%	14	31.1%	4	50.0%	4	16.7%	5	25.0%	6	37.5%	7	31.8%	26	28.9%
6-10 years	0	0.0%	18	22.0%	11	24.4%	7	15.6%	2	25.0%	3	12.5%	3	15.0%	3	18.8%	7	31.8%	18	20.0%
11-15 years	1	12.5%	7	8.5%	2	4.4%	6	13.3%	1	12.5%	3	12.5%	2	10.0%	0	0.0%	2	9.1%	8	8.9%
16-20 years	0	0.0%	4	4.9%	1	2.2%	3	6.7%	0	0.0%	2	8.3%	0	0.0%	1	6.3%	1	4.5%	4	4.4%
More than 20 years	1	12.5%	5	6.1%	3	6.7%	3	6.7%	1	12.5%	2	8.3%	0	0.0%	2	12.5%	1	4.5%	6	6.7%
Total	8	100.0%	82	100.0%	45	100.0%	45	100.0%	8	100.0%	24	100.0%	20	100.0%	16	100.0%	22	100.0%	90	100.0%
Q21. Please select the three most important objectives for this initiative: (Select all that apply)																				
Academic planning	3	37.5%	17	20.7%	11	24.4%	9	20.0%	4	50.0%	8	33.3%	2	10.0%	4	25.0%	2	9.1%	20	22.2%
Academic success strategies	2	25.0%	19	23.2%	14	31.1%	7	15.6%	0	0.0%	6	25.0%	4	20.0%	3	18.8%	8	36.4%	21	23.3%
Analytical, critical-thinking, or problem-solving skills	1	12.5%	8	9.8%	4	8.9%	5	11.1%	1	12.5%	2	8.3%	3	15.0%	1	6.3%	2	9.1%	9	10.0%
Career exploration and/or preparation	4	50.0%	24	29.3%	15	33.3%	13	28.9%	4	50.0%	5	20.8%	6	30.0%	6	37.5%	7	31.8%	28	31.1%
Civic engagement	0	0.0%	3	3.7%	2	4.4%	1	2.2%	0	0.0%	0	0.0%	2	10.0%	0	0.0%	1	4.5%	3	3.3%

Table continues on page 97

Table continued from page 96

Q21. Please select the three most important objectives for this initiative: (Select all that apply)

Survey question/ responses	Institutional type				Institution control				Number of undergraduates enrolled										Total	
	Two-year		Four-year		Public		Private		Fewer than 1,000		1,001-2,500		2,501-5,000		5,001-10,000		More than 10,000			
	Freq.	%	Freq	%	Freq.	%	Freq.	%	Freq.	%	Freq.	%	Freq.	%	Freq.	%	Freq.	%	Freq.	%
Common sophomore-year experience	2	25.0%	20	24.4%	7	15.6%	15	33.3%	1	12.5%	8	33.3%	6	30.0%	2	12.5%	5	22.7%	22	24.4%
Connection with the institution or campus	1	12.5%	30	36.6%	12	26.7%	19	42.2%	4	50.0%	6	25.0%	6	30.0%	8	50.0%	7	31.8%	31	34.4%
Developmental education, remediation, and/or review	0	0.0%	2	2.4%	1	2.2%	1	2.2%	0	0.0%	2	8.3%	0	0.0%	0	0.0%	0	0.0%	2	2.2%
Digital literacy	0	0.0%	0	0.0%	0	0.0%	0	0.0%	0	0.0%	0	0.0%	0	0.0%	0	0.0%	0	0.0%	0	0.0%
Discipline-specific knowledge	2	25.0%	2	2.4%	2	4.4%	2	4.4%	1	12.5%	0	0.0%	2	10.0%	0	0.0%	1	4.5%	4	4.4%
Graduate or professional school preparation (e.g., premed, prelaw)	0	0.0%	4	4.9%	1	2.2%	3	6.7%	0	0.0%	2	8.3%	0	0.0%	1	6.3%	1	4.5%	4	4.4%
Health and wellness	0	0.0%	2	2.4%	1	2.2%	1	2.2%	0	0.0%	0	0.0%	1	5.0%	1	6.3%	0	0.0%	2	2.2%
Information literacy	0	0.0%	0	0.0%	0	0.0%	0	0.0%	0	0.0%	0	0.0%	0	0.0%	0	0.0%	0	0.0%	0	0.0%
Integrative and applied learning	0	0.0%	5	6.1%	1	2.2%	4	8.9%	0	0.0%	1	4.2%	4	20.0%	0	0.0%	0	0.0%	5	5.6%
Intercultural competence, diversity skills, or engaging with different perspectives	1	12.5%	2	2.4%	0	0.0%	3	6.7%	1	12.5%	2	8.3%	0	0.0%	0	0.0%	0	0.0%	3	3.3%
Introduction to a major, discipline, or career path	0	0.0%	10	12.2%	6	13.3%	4	8.9%	0	0.0%	1	4.2%	3	15.0%	3	18.8%	3	13.6%	10	11.1%

Table continues on page 98

Table continued from page 97

Q21. Please select the three most important objectives for this initiative: (Select all that apply)

Survey question/ responses	Institutional type				Institution control				Number of undergraduates enrolled										Total	
	Two-year		Four-year		Public		Private		Fewer than 1,000		1,001-2,500		2,501-5,000		5,001-10,000		More than 10,000			
	Freq.	%	Freq	%	Freq.	%	Freq.	%	Freq.	%	Freq.	%	Freq.	%	Freq.	%	Freq.	%	Freq.	%
Introduction to college-level academic expectations	0	0.0%	2	2.4%	2	4.4%	0	0.0%	0	0.0%	0	0.0%	2	10.0%	0	0.0%	0	0.0%	2	2.2%
Introduction to the liberal arts	0	0.0%	0	0.0%	0	0.0%	0	0.0%	0	0.0%	0	0.0%	0	0.0%	0	0.0%	0	0.0%	0	0.0%
Knowledge of institution or campus resources and services	0	0.0%	11	13.4%	6	13.3%	5	11.1%	0	0.0%	4	16.7%	0	0.0%	3	18.8%	4	18.2%	11	12.2%
Major exploration	1	12.5%	13	15.9%	6	13.3%	8	17.8%	3	37.5%	2	8.3%	4	20.0%	2	12.5%	3	13.6%	14	15.6%
Oral communication skills	0	0.0%	4	4.9%	1	2.2%	3	6.7%	0	0.0%	2	8.3%	0	0.0%	1	6.3%	1	4.5%	4	4.4%
Persistence, retention, or third-year return rates	3	37.5%	23	28.0%	19	42.2%	7	15.6%	2	25.0%	6	25.0%	6	30.0%	7	43.8%	5	22.7%	26	28.9%
Personal exploration or development	0	0.0%	0	0.0%	0	0.0%	0	0.0%	0	0.0%	0	0.0%	0	0.0%	0	0.0%	0	0.0%	0	0.0%
Project planning, teamwork, or management skills	0	0.0%	0	0.0%	0	0.0%	0	0.0%	0	0.0%	0	0.0%	0	0.0%	0	0.0%	0	0.0%	0	0.0%
Social support networks (e.g., friendships)	0	0.0%	10	12.2%	5	11.1%	5	11.1%	0	0.0%	2	8.3%	2	10.0%	2	12.5%	4	18.2%	10	11.1%
Student-faculty interaction	0	0.0%	10	12.2%	3	6.7%	7	15.6%	1	12.5%	3	12.5%	4	20.0%	0	0.0%	2	9.1%	10	11.1%
Writing skills	0	0.0%	2	2.4%	1	2.2%	1	2.2%	0	0.0%	1	4.2%	0	0.0%	0	0.0%	1	4.5%	2	2.2%

Table continues on page 99

Table continued from page 98

Survey question/ responses	Institutional type				Institution control				Number of undergraduates enrolled										Total	
	Two-year		Four-year		Public		Private		Fewer than 1,000		1,001-2,500		2,501-5,000		5,001-10,000		More than 10,000			
	Freq.	%	Freq.	%	Freq.	%	Freq.	%	Freq.	%	Freq.	%	Freq.	%	Freq.	%	Freq.	%	Freq.	%
Q21. Please select the three most important objectives for this initiative: (Select all that apply)																				
Other, please specify	1	12.5%	4	4.9%	3	6.7%	2	4.4%	0	0.0%	2	8.3%	0	0.0%	1	6.3%	2	9.1%	5	5.6%
Total	8	100.0%	82	100.0%	45	100.0%	45	100.0%	8	100.0%	24	100.0%	20	100.0%	16	100.0%	22	100.0%	90	100.0%
Q22. To what extent are each of the following elements present in this initiative? - Performance expectations set at appropriately high levels																				
1 - Element is not present	2	25.0%	32	39.0%	15	33.3%	19	42.2%	2	25.0%	10	41.7%	6	30.0%	9	56.3%	7	31.8%	34	37.8%
2	0	0.0%	9	11.0%	4	8.9%	5	11.1%	0	0.0%	2	8.3%	3	15.0%	2	12.5%	2	9.1%	9	10.0%
3 - Element is partially present	4	50.0%	18	22.0%	11	24.4%	11	24.4%	6	75.0%	6	25.0%	3	15.0%	2	12.5%	5	22.7%	22	24.4%
4	1	12.5%	10	12.2%	7	15.6%	4	8.9%	0	0.0%	3	12.5%	3	15.0%	2	12.5%	3	13.6%	11	12.2%
5 - Element is pervasive throughout initiative	1	12.5%	13	15.9%	8	17.8%	6	13.3%	0	0.0%	3	12.5%	5	25.0%	1	6.3%	5	22.7%	14	15.6%
Total	8	100.0%	82	100.0%	45	100.0%	45	100.0%	8	100.0%	24	100.0%	20	100.0%	16	100.0%	22	100.0%	90	100.0%
Q23. To what extent are each of the following elements present in this initiative? - Significance investment of time and effort by students over an extended period of time																				
1 - Element is not present	1	12.5%	23	28.0%	8	17.8%	16	35.6%	2	25.0%	8	33.3%	3	15.0%	7	43.8%	4	18.2%	24	26.7%
2	3	37.5%	8	9.8%	8	17.8%	3	6.7%	1	12.5%	4	16.7%	2	10.0%	3	18.8%	1	4.5%	11	12.2%
3 - Element is partially present	2	25.0%	20	24.4%	14	31.1%	8	17.8%	3	37.5%	2	8.3%	6	30.0%	2	12.5%	9	40.9%	22	24.4%
4	1	12.5%	19	23.2%	10	22.2%	10	22.2%	1	12.5%	7	29.2%	5	25.0%	2	12.5%	5	22.7%	20	22.2%
5 - Element is pervasive throughout initiative	1	12.5%	12	14.6%	5	11.1%	8	17.8%	1	12.5%	3	12.5%	4	20.0%	2	12.5%	3	13.6%	13	14.4%
Total	8	100.0%	82	100.0%	45	100.0%	45	100.0%	8	100.0%	24	100.0%	20	100.0%	16	100.0%	22	100.0%	90	100.0%

Table continues on page 100

Table continued from page 99

Survey question/ responses	Institutional type				Institution control				Number of undergraduates enrolled										Total	
	Two-year		Four-year		Public		Private		Fewer than 1,000		1,001-2,500		2,501-5,000		5,001-10,000		More than 10,000			
	Freq.	%	Freq	%	Freq.	%	Freq.	%	Freq.	%	Freq.	%	Freq.	%	Freq.	%	Freq.	%	Freq.	%
Q24. To what extent are each of the following elements present in this initiative? - Interactions with faculty and peers about substantive matters																				
1 - Element is not present	1	12.5%	13	15.9%	7	15.6%	7	15.6%	0	0.0%	3	12.5%	1	5.0%	5	31.3%	5	22.7%	14	15.6%
2	1	12.5%	4	4.9%	1	2.2%	4	8.9%	0	0.0%	2	8.3%	0	0.0%	3	18.8%	0	0.0%	5	5.6%
3 - Element is partially present	2	25.0%	23	28.0%	14	31.1%	11	24.4%	3	37.5%	6	25.0%	6	30.0%	3	18.8%	7	31.8%	25	27.8%
4	3	37.5%	19	23.2%	12	26.7%	10	22.2%	3	37.5%	5	20.8%	7	35.0%	2	12.5%	5	22.7%	22	24.4%
5 - Element is pervasive throughout initiative	1	12.5%	23	28.0%	11	24.4%	13	28.9%	2	25.0%	8	33.3%	6	30.0%	3	18.8%	5	22.7%	24	26.7%
Total	8	100.0%	82	100.0%	45	100.0%	45	100.0%	8	100.0%	24	100.0%	20	100.0%	16	100.0%	22	100.0%	90	100.0%
Q25. To what extent are each of the following elements present in this initiative? - Experiences with diversity, wherein students are exposed to and must content with people and circumstances that differ from those with which students are familiar																				
1 - Element is not present	2	25.0%	22	26.8%	10	22.2%	14	31.1%	2	25.0%	6	25.0%	3	15.0%	7	43.8%	6	27.3%	24	26.7%
2	0	0.0%	13	15.9%	8	17.8%	5	11.1%	1	12.5%	2	8.3%	4	20.0%	2	12.5%	4	18.2%	13	14.4%
3 - Element is partially present	4	50.0%	18	22.0%	9	20.0%	13	28.9%	3	37.5%	10	41.7%	5	25.0%	1	6.3%	3	13.6%	22	24.4%
4	1	12.5%	14	17.1%	10	22.2%	5	11.1%	1	12.5%	3	12.5%	6	30.0%	2	12.5%	3	13.6%	15	16.7%
5 - Element is pervasive throughout initiative	1	12.5%	15	18.3%	8	17.8%	8	17.8%	1	12.5%	3	12.5%	2	10.0%	4	25.0%	6	27.3%	16	17.8%
Total	8	100.0%	82	100.0%	45	100.0%	45	100.0%	8	100.0%	24	100.0%	20	100.0%	16	100.0%	22	100.0%	90	100.0%
Q26. To what extent are each of the following elements present in this initiative? - Frequent, timely, and constructive feedback																				
1 - Element is not present	1	12.5%	22	26.8%	9	20.0%	14	31.1%	3	37.5%	6	25.0%	2	10.0%	6	37.5%	6	27.3%	23	25.6%
2	1	12.5%	11	13.4%	6	13.3%	6	13.3%	1	12.5%	2	8.3%	3	15.0%	4	25.0%	2	9.1%	12	13.3%

Table continues on page 101

Table continued from page 100

Survey question/responses	Institutional type				Institution control				Number of undergraduates enrolled											Total	
	Two-year		Four-year		Public		Private		Fewer than 1,000		1,001-2,500		2,501-5,000		5,001-10,000		More than 10,000					
	Freq.	%	Freq.	%	Freq.	%	Freq.	%	Freq.	%	Freq.	%	Freq.	%	Freq.	%	Freq.	%	Freq.	%
Q26. To what extent are each of the following elements present in this initiative? - Frequent, timely, and constructive feedback																				
3 - Element is partially present	3	37.5%	19	23.2%	10	22.2%	12	26.7%	1	12.5%	8	33.3%	9	45.0%	2	12.5%	2	9.1%	22	24.4%
4	3	37.5%	13	15.9%	10	22.2%	6	13.3%	3	37.5%	3	12.5%	3	15.0%	2	12.5%	5	22.7%	16	17.8%
5 - Element is pervasive throughout initiative	0	0.0%	17	20.7%	10	22.2%	7	15.6%	0	0.0%	5	20.8%	3	15.0%	2	12.5%	7	31.8%	17	18.9%
Total	8	100.0%	82	100.0%	45	100.0%	45	100.0%	8	100.0%	24	100.0%	20	100.0%	16	100.0%	22	100.0%	90	100.0%
Q27. To what extent are each of the following elements present in this initiative? - Periodic, structured opportunities to reflect and integrate learning																				
1 - Element is not present	1	12.5%	20	24.4%	9	20.0%	12	26.7%	1	12.5%	3	12.5%	3	15.0%	9	56.3%	5	22.7%	21	23.3%
2	0	0.0%	6	7.3%	2	4.4%	4	8.9%	2	25.0%	1	4.2%	1	5.0%	1	6.3%	1	4.5%	6	6.7%
3 - Element is partially present	2	25.0%	20	24.4%	13	28.9%	9	20.0%	2	25.0%	6	25.0%	7	35.0%	3	18.8%	4	18.2%	22	24.4%
4	4	50.0%	20	24.4%	14	31.1%	10	22.2%	2	25.0%	8	33.3%	6	30.0%	2	12.5%	6	27.3%	24	26.7%
5 - Element is pervasive throughout initiative	1	12.5%	16	19.5%	7	15.6%	10	22.2%	1	12.5%	6	25.0%	3	15.0%	1	6.3%	6	27.3%	17	18.9%
Total	8	100.0%	82	100.0%	45	100.0%	45	100.0%	8	100.0%	24	100.0%	20	100.0%	16	100.0%	22	100.0%	90	100.0%
Q28. To what extent are each of the following elements present in this initiative? - Opportunities to discover relevance of learning through real-world applications																				
1 - Element is not present	1	12.5%	17	20.7%	8	17.8%	10	22.2%	3	37.5%	3	12.5%	3	15.0%	5	31.3%	4	18.2%	18	20.0%
2	0	0.0%	10	12.2%	4	8.9%	6	13.3%	0	0.0%	4	16.7%	2	10.0%	1	6.3%	3	13.6%	10	11.1%
3 - Element is partially present	1	12.5%	24	29.3%	17	37.8%	8	17.8%	2	25.0%	6	25.0%	4	20.0%	4	25.0%	9	40.9%	25	27.8%
4	5	62.5%	16	19.5%	10	22.2%	11	24.4%	2	25.0%	5	20.8%	6	30.0%	5	31.3%	3	13.6%	21	23.3%

Table continues on page 102

Table continued from page 101

Survey question/ responses	Institutional type				Institution control				Number of undergraduates enrolled										Total	
	Two-year		Four-year		Public		Private		Fewer than 1,000		1,001-2,500		2,501-5,000		5,001-10,000		More than 10,000			
	Freq.	%	Freq	%	Freq.	%	Freq.	%	Freq.	%	Freq.	%	Freq.	%	Freq.	%	Freq.	%	Freq.	%
Q28. To what extent are each of the following elements present in this initiative? - Opportunities to discover relevance of learning through real-world applications																				
5 - Element is pervasive throughout initiative	1	12.5%	15	18.3%	6	13.3%	10	22.2%	1	12.5%	6	25.0%	5	25.0%	1	6.3%	3	13.6%	16	17.8%
Total	8	100.0%	82	100.0%	45	100.0%	45	100.0%	8	100.0%	24	100.0%	20	100.0%	16	100.0%	22	100.0%	90	100.0%
Q29. To what extent are each of the following elements present in this initiative? - Public demonstration of competence																				
1 - Element is not present	3	37.5%	39	47.6%	18	40.0%	24	53.3%	3	37.5%	11	45.8%	8	40.0%	12	75.0%	8	36.4%	42	46.7%
2	0	0.0%	12	14.6%	9	20.0%	3	6.7%	0	0.0%	2	8.3%	2	10.0%	1	6.3%	7	31.8%	12	13.3%
3 - Element is partially present	2	25.0%	14	17.1%	9	20.0%	7	15.6%	3	37.5%	4	16.7%	3	15.0%	2	12.5%	4	18.2%	16	17.8%
4	2	25.0%	11	13.4%	6	13.3%	7	15.6%	1	12.5%	6	25.0%	5	25.0%	0	0.0%	1	4.5%	13	14.4%
5 - Element is pervasive throughout initiative	1	12.5%	6	7.3%	3	6.7%	4	8.9%	1	12.5%	1	4.2%	2	10.0%	1	6.3%	2	9.1%	7	7.8%
Total	8	100.0%	82	100.0%	45	100.0%	45	100.0%	8	100.0%	24	100.0%	20	100.0%	16	100.0%	22	100.0%	90	100.0%
Q30. Which campus unit directly administers this initiative?																				
Academic affairs central office	0	0.0%	13	15.9%	3	6.7%	10	22.2%	2	25.0%	7	29.2%	2	10.0%	1	6.3%	1	4.5%	13	14.4%
Academic department(s)	1	12.5%	4	4.9%	3	6.7%	2	4.4%	0	0.0%	0	0.0%	1	5.0%	3	18.8%	1	4.5%	5	5.6%
College or school (e.g., College of Liberal Arts)	0	0.0%	2	2.4%	1	2.2%	1	2.2%	0	0.0%	1	4.2%	1	5.0%	0	0.0%	0	0.0%	2	2.2%
Sophomore-year program office	0	0.0%	8	9.8%	6	13.3%	2	4.4%	1	12.5%	2	8.3%	0	0.0%	2	12.5%	3	13.6%	8	8.9%
Student affairs central office	4	50.0%	16	19.5%	11	24.4%	9	20.0%	4	50.0%	4	16.7%	6	30.0%	2	12.5%	4	18.2%	20	22.2%

Table continues on page 103

Table continued from page 102

Survey question/responses	Two-year Freq.	%	Four-year Freq.	%	Public Freq.	%	Private Freq.	%	Fewer than 1,000 Freq.	%	1,001-2,500 Freq.	%	2,501-5,000 Freq.	%	5,001-10,000 Freq.	%	More than 10,000 Freq.	%	Total Freq.	%
Q30. Which campus unit directly administers this initiative?																				
University college	0	0.0%	2	2.4%	0	0.0%	2	4.4%	0	0.0%	0	0.0%	1	5.0%	1	6.3%	0	0.0%	2	2.2%
Other	3	37.5%	37	45.1%	21	46.7%	19	42.2%	1	12.5%	10	41.7%	9	45.0%	7	43.8%	13	59.1%	40	44.4%
Total	8	100.0%	82	100.0%	45	100.0%	45	100.0%	8	100.0%	24	100.0%	20	100.0%	16	100.0%	22	100.0%	90	100.0%
Q31. How is this initiative primarily funded?																				
Auxiliary funds	0	0.0%	15	18.3%	7	15.6%	8	17.8%	0	0.0%	2	8.3%	4	20.0%	4	25.0%	5	22.7%	15	16.7%
Foundation funds	0	0.0%	2	2.4%	1	2.2%	1	2.2%	0	0.0%	1	4.2%	1	5.0%	0	0.0%	0	0.0%	2	2.2%
Grant funds	4	50.0%	6	7.3%	6	13.3%	4	8.9%	1	12.5%	5	20.8%	1	5.0%	1	6.3%	2	9.1%	10	11.1%
Nonrecurring or one-time funds	0	0.0%	2	2.4%	0	0.0%	2	4.4%	0	0.0%	0	0.0%	1	5.0%	1	6.3%	0	0.0%	2	2.2%
Recurring state- or university-appropriated funds	1	12.5%	24	29.3%	18	40.0%	7	15.6%	1	12.5%	6	25.0%	4	20.0%	6	37.5%	8	36.4%	25	27.8%
Student activity fees	1	12.5%	2	2.4%	1	2.2%	2	4.4%	1	12.5%	0	0.0%	1	5.0%	0	0.0%	1	4.5%	3	3.3%
Tuition revenue	0	0.0%	18	22.0%	5	11.1%	13	28.9%	4	50.0%	6	25.0%	4	20.0%	2	12.5%	2	9.1%	18	20.0%
Other	2	25.0%	13	15.9%	7	15.6%	8	17.8%	1	12.5%	4	16.7%	4	20.0%	2	12.5%	4	18.2%	15	16.7%
Total	8	100.0%	82	100.0%	45	100.0%	45	100.0%	8	100.0%	24	100.0%	20	100.0%	16	100.0%	22	100.0%	90	100.0%
Q32. Has this initiative been formally assessed or evaluated in the past three years?																				
Yes	3	37.5%	39	47.6%	24	53.3%	18	40.0%	2	25.0%	10	41.7%	7	35.0%	9	56.3%	14	63.6%	42	46.7%
No	3	37.5%	33	40.2%	17	37.8%	19	42.2%	4	50.0%	11	45.8%	12	60.0%	3	18.8%	6	27.3%	36	40.0%
I don't know	2	25.0%	10	12.2%	4	8.9%	8	17.8%	2	25.0%	3	12.5%	1	5.0%	4	25.0%	2	9.1%	12	13.3%
Total	8	100.0%	82	100.0%	45	100.0%	45	100.0%	8	100.0%	24	100.0%	20	100.0%	16	100.0%	22	100.0%	90	100.0%

Table continues on page 104

Table continued from page 103

Q33. What type of assessment was conducted? (Select all that apply)

Survey question/responses	Institutional type				Institution control				Number of undergraduates enrolled										Total	
	Two-year		Four-year		Public		Private		Fewer than 1,000		1,001-2,500		2,501-5,000		5,001-10,000		More than 10,000			
	Freq.	%	Freq.	%	Freq.	%	Freq.	%	Freq.	%	Freq.	%	Freq.	%	Freq.	%	Freq.	%	Freq.	%
Analysis of institutional data (e.g., GPA, retentional rates, graduation)	3	100.0%	24	61.5%	11	45.8%	16	88.9%	2	100.0%	6	60.0%	4	57.1%	8	88.9%	7	50.0%	27	64.3%
Direct assessment of student learning outcomes	2	66.7%	12	30.8%	8	33.3%	6	33.3%	1	50.0%	5	50.0%	2	28.6%	1	11.1%	5	35.7%	14	33.3%
Focus groups with faculty	0	0.0%	3	7.7%	1	4.2%	2	11.1%	0	0.0%	2	20.0%	0	0.0%	0	0.0%	1	7.1%	3	7.1%
Focus groups with professional staff	0	0.0%	1	2.6%	1	4.2%	0	0.0%	0	0.0%	0	0.0%	0	0.0%	0	0.0%	1	7.1%	1	2.4%
Focus groups with students	0	0.0%	10	25.6%	6	25.0%	4	22.2%	1	50.0%	3	30.0%	1	14.3%	2	22.2%	3	21.4%	10	23.8%
Individual interviews with faculty	0	0.0%	3	7.7%	2	8.3%	1	5.6%	0	0.0%	1	10.0%	0	0.0%	1	11.1%	1	7.1%	3	7.1%
Individual interviews with orientation staff	0	0.0%	1	2.6%	1	4.2%	0	0.0%	0	0.0%	0	0.0%	0	0.0%	0	0.0%	1	7.1%	1	2.4%
Individual interviews with students	1	33.3%	9	23.1%	6	25.0%	4	22.2%	0	0.0%	1	10.0%	3	42.9%	3	33.3%	3	21.4%	10	23.8%
Program review	1	33.3%	13	33.3%	7	29.2%	7	38.9%	1	50.0%	3	30.0%	2	28.6%	5	55.6%	3	21.4%	14	33.3%
Student course evaluation	1	33.3%	8	20.5%	5	20.8%	4	22.2%	0	0.0%	3	30.0%	2	28.6%	1	11.1%	3	21.4%	9	21.4%
Survey instrument - Locally designed	2	66.7%	20	51.3%	14	58.3%	8	44.4%	0	0.0%	5	50.0%	3	42.9%	6	66.7%	8	57.1%	22	52.4%
Survey instrument - Nationally available	1	33.3%	3	7.7%	3	12.5%	1	5.6%	0	0.0%	0	0.0%	2	28.6%	0	0.0%	2	14.3%	4	9.5%
Other	0	0.0%	1	2.6%	1	4.2%	0	0.0%	0	0.0%	0	0.0%	0	0.0%	0	0.0%	1	7.1%	1	2.4%
Total	3	100.0%	39	100.0%	24	100.0%	18	100.0%	2	100.0%	10	100.0%	7	100.0%	9	100.0%	14	100.0%	42	100.0%

Table continues on page 105

Table continued from page 104

Survey question/ responses	Institutional type				Institution control				Number of undergraduates enrolled										Total	
	Two-year		Four-year		Public		Private		Fewer than 1,000		1,001-2,500		2,501-5,000		5,001-10,000		More than 10,000			
	Freq.	%	Freq	%	Freq.	%	Freq.	%	Freq.	%	Freq.	%	Freq.	%	Freq.	%	Freq.	%	Freq.	%
Q34. Please identify the student learning outcomes you assessed: (Select all that apply)																				
Academic planning	1	50.0%	4	36.4%	4	50.0%	1	20.0%	1	100.0%	1	25.0%	0	0.0%	1	100.0%	2	40.0%	5	38.5%
Academic success strategies	0	0.0%	3	27.3%	2	25.0%	1	20.0%	0	0.0%	0	0.0%	0	0.0%	1	100.0%	2	40.0%	3	23.1%
Analytical, critical-thinking, or problem-solving skills	0	0.0%	2	18.2%	1	12.5%	1	20.0%	0	0.0%	0	0.0%	0	0.0%	1	100.0%	1	20.0%	2	15.4%
Career exploration and/or preparation	1	50.0%	6	54.5%	4	50.0%	3	60.0%	0	0.0%	2	50.0%	1	50.0%	1	100.0%	3	60.0%	7	53.8%
Civic engagement	0	0.0%	2	18.2%	1	12.5%	1	20.0%	0	0.0%	0	0.0%	0	0.0%	1	100.0%	1	20.0%	2	15.4%
Common sophomore-year experience	0	0.0%	2	18.2%	0	0.0%	2	40.0%	0	0.0%	1	25.0%	0	0.0%	1	100.0%	0	0.0%	2	15.4%
Connection with the institution or campus	1	50.0%	6	54.5%	5	62.5%	2	40.0%	1	100.0%	1	25.0%	1	50.0%	1	100.0%	3	60.0%	7	53.8%
Developmental education, remediation, and/or review	0	0.0%	1	9.1%	0	0.0%	1	20.0%	0	0.0%	0	0.0%	0	0.0%	1	100.0%	0	0.0%	1	7.7%
Digital literacy	0	0.0%	1	9.1%	0	0.0%	1	20.0%	0	0.0%	0	0.0%	0	0.0%	1	100.0%	0	0.0%	1	7.7%
Discipline-specific knowledge	1	50.0%	3	27.3%	1	12.5%	3	60.0%	0	0.0%	1	25.0%	2	100.0%	1	100.0%	0	0.0%	4	30.8%
Graduate or professional school preparation (e.g., premed, prelaw)	0	0.0%	2	18.2%	0	0.0%	2	40.0%	0	0.0%	1	25.0%	0	0.0%	1	100.0%	0	0.0%	2	15.4%
Health and wellness	0	0.0%	2	18.2%	1	12.5%	1	20.0%	0	0.0%	0	0.0%	0	0.0%	1	100.0%	1	20.0%	2	15.4%
Information literacy	0	0.0%	1	9.1%	0	0.0%	1	20.0%	0	0.0%	0	0.0%	0	0.0%	1	100.0%	0	0.0%	1	7.7%

Table continues on page 106

Table continued from page 105

Q34. Please identify the student learning outcomes you assessed: (Select all that apply)

Survey question/ responses	Institutional type				Institution control				Number of undergraduates enrolled										Total	
	Two-year		Four-year		Public		Private		Fewer than 1,000		1,001-2,500		2,501-5,000		5,001-10,000		More than 10,000			
	Freq.	%	Freq.	%	Freq.	%	Freq.	%	Freq.	%	Freq.	%	Freq.	%	Freq.	%	Freq.	%	Freq.	%
Integrative and applied learning	0	0.0%	3	27.3%	1	12.5%	2	40.0%	0	0.0%	0	0.0%	1	50.0%	1	100.0%	1	20.0%	3	23.1%
Intercultural competence, diversity skills, or engaging with different perspectives	0	0.0%	4	36.4%	2	25.0%	2	40.0%	0	0.0%	0	0.0%	1	50.0%	1	100.0%	2	40.0%	4	30.8%
Introduction to a major, discipline, or career path	0	0.0%	3	27.3%	1	12.5%	2	40.0%	0	0.0%	1	25.0%	0	0.0%	1	100.0%	1	20.0%	3	23.1%
Introduction to college-level academic expectations	0	0.0%	1	9.1%	0	0.0%	1	20.0%	0	0.0%	0	0.0%	0	0.0%	1	100.0%	0	0.0%	1	7.7%
Introduction to the liberal arts	0	0.0%	1	9.1%	0	0.0%	1	20.0%	0	0.0%	0	0.0%	0	0.0%	1	100.0%	0	0.0%	1	7.7%
Knowledge of institution or campus resources and services	0	0.0%	6	54.5%	5	62.5%	1	20.0%	1	100.0%	0	0.0%	0	0.0%	1	100.0%	4	80.0%	6	46.2%
Major exploration	0	0.0%	2	18.2%	0	0.0%	2	40.0%	0	0.0%	1	25.0%	0	0.0%	1	100.0%	0	0.0%	2	15.4%
Oral communication skills	0	0.0%	3	27.3%	0	0.0%	3	60.0%	0	0.0%	1	25.0%	1	50.0%	1	100.0%	0	0.0%	3	23.1%
Persistence, retention, or third-year return rates	2	100.0%	7	63.6%	6	75.0%	3	60.0%	0	0.0%	3	75.0%	1	50.0%	1	100.0%	4	80.0%	9	69.2%
Personal exploration or development	1	50.0%	5	45.5%	3	37.5%	3	60.0%	0	0.0%	2	50.0%	1	50.0%	1	100.0%	2	40.0%	6	46.2%
Project planning, teamwork, or management skills	0	0.0%	2	18.2%	1	12.5%	1	20.0%	0	0.0%	0	0.0%	0	0.0%	1	100.0%	1	20.0%	2	15.4%

Table continues on page 107

Table continued from page 106

Survey question/ responses	Institutional type				Institution control				Number of undergraduates enrolled											
	Two-year		Four-year		Public		Private		Fewer than 1,000		1,001-2,500		2,501-5,000		5,001-10,000		More than 10,000		Total	
	Freq.	%	Freq.	%	Freq.	%	Freq.	%	Freq.	%	Freq.	%	Freq.	%	Freq.	%	Freq.	%	Freq.	%
Q34. Please identify the student learning outcomes you assessed: (Select all that apply)																				
Social support networks (e.g., friendships)	0	0.0%	3	27.3%	2	25.0%	1	20.0%	0	0.0%	0	0.0%	0	0.0%	1	100.0%	2	40.0%	3	23.1%
Student-faculty interaction	0	0.0%	4	36.4%	2	25.0%	2	40.0%	0	0.0%	1	25.0%	0	0.0%	1	100.0%	2	40.0%	4	30.8%
Writing skills	0	0.0%	3	27.3%	1	12.5%	2	40.0%	0	0.0%	1	25.0%	0	0.0%	1	100.0%	1	20.0%	3	23.1%
Other	0	0.0%	2	18.2%	2	25.0%	0	0.0%	0	0.0%	0	0.0%	0	0.0%	0	0.0%	2	40.0%	2	15.4%
Total	2	100.0%	11	100.0%	8	100.0%	5	100.0%	1	100.0%	4	100.0%	2	100.0%	1	100.0%	5	100.0%	13	100.0%
Q35. Please identify the national survey(s) you used: (Select all that apply) - From Q33 (Direct assessment of student learning outcomes)																				
College Student Experiences Questionnaire (CSEQ)	0	0.0%	0	0.0%	0	0.0%	0	0.0%	0	0.0%	0	–	0	0.0%	0	–	0	0.0%	0	0.0%
Collegiate Learning Assessment (CLA)	0	0.0%	0	0.0%	0	0.0%	0	0.0%	0	0.0%	0	–	0	0.0%	0	–	0	0.0%	0	0.0%
Community College Survey of Student Engagement (CCSSE)	1	100.0%	0	0.0%	1	33.3%	0	0.0%	0	0.0%	0	–	1	50.0%	0	–	0	0.0%	1	25.0%
Diverse Learning Environments Study (DLE; Administered by HERI at UCLA)	0	0.0%	0	0.0%	0	0.0%	0	0.0%	0	0.0%	0	–	0	0.0%	0	–	0	0.0%	0	0.0%
Faculty Survey of Student Engagement (FSSE)	1	100.0%	0	0.0%	1	33.3%	0	0.0%	0	0.0%	0	–	1	50.0%	0	–	0	0.0%	1	25.0%
Individual Developmental and Educational Assessment (IDEA)	0	0.0%	0	0.0%	0	0.0%	0	0.0%	0	0.0%	0	–	0	0.0%	0	–	0	0.0%	0	0.0%

Table continues on page 108

Table continued from page 107

Survey question/responses	Institutional type				Institution control				Number of undergraduates enrolled										Total	
	Two-year		Four-year		Public		Private		Fewer than 1,000		1,001-2,500		2,501-5,000		5,001-10,000		More than 10,000			
	Freq.	%	Freq.	%	Freq.	%	Freq.	%	Freq.	%	Freq.	%	Freq.	%	Freq.	%	Freq.	%	Freq.	%
Q35. Please identify the national survey(s) you used: (Select all that apply) - From Q33 (Direct assessment of student learning outcomes)																				
National Survey of Student Engagement (NSSE)	0	0.0%	2	66.7%	1	33.3%	1	100.0%	0	–	0	–	1	50.0%	0	–	1	20.0%	1	25.0%
Second-Year Student Assessment (Noel-Levitz)	0	0.0%	0	0.0%	0	0.0%	0	0.0%	0	–	0	–	0	0.0%	0	–	0	0.0%	0	0.0%
Sophomore Experiences Survey (www.thrivingincollege.org)	0	0.0%	0	0.0%	0	0.0%	0	0.0%	0	–	0	–	0	0.0%	0	–	0	0.0%	0	0.0%
Student Satisfaction Inventory (SSI)	0	0.0%	1	33.3%	1	33.3%	0	0.0%	0	–	0	–	0	0.0%	0	–	1	20.0%	1	25.0%
Other	0	0.0%	2	66.7%	1	33.3%	1	100.0%	0	–	0	–	1	50.0%	0	–	1	20.0%	2	50.0%
Total	1	100.0%	3	100.0%	3	100.0%	1	100.0%	0	–	0	–	2	100.0%	0	–	5	100.0%	4	100.0%
Q36. What is the approximate percentage of sophomore students reached by academic advising for sophomores on your campus?																				
10% or less	0	0.0%	0	0.0%	0	0.0%	0	0.0%	0	0.0%	0	0.0%	0	0.0%	0	0.0%	0	0.0%	0	0.0%
11-20%	0	0.0%	0	0.0%	0	0.0%	0	0.0%	0	0.0%	0	0.0%	0	0.0%	0	0.0%	0	0.0%	0	0.0%
21-30%	0	0.0%	0	0.0%	0	0.0%	0	0.0%	0	0.0%	0	0.0%	0	0.0%	0	0.0%	0	0.0%	0	0.0%
31-40%	0	0.0%	1	1.9%	0	0.0%	1	3.8%	1	14.3%	0	0.0%	0	0.0%	0	0.0%	0	0.0%	1	1.6%
41-50%	1	12.5%	0	0.0%	1	3.0%	0	0.0%	0	0.0%	1	7.1%	0	0.0%	0	0.0%	0	0.0%	1	1.6%
51-60%	1	12.5%	2	3.8%	3	9.1%	0	0.0%	0	0.0%	0	0.0%	0	0.0%	1	7.7%	2	10.5%	3	4.9%
61-70%	2	25.0%	1	1.9%	3	9.1%	0	0.0%	0	0.0%	0	0.0%	1	12.5%	1	7.7%	1	5.3%	3	4.9%
71-80%	1	12.5%	4	7.5%	3	9.1%	2	7.7%	0	0.0%	0	0.0%	2	25.0%	0	0.0%	3	15.8%	5	8.2%
81-90%	2	25.0%	4	7.5%	4	12.1%	1	3.8%	0	0.0%	1	7.1%	2	25.0%	0	0.0%	3	15.8%	6	9.8%

Table continues on page 109

Table continued from page 108

Survey question/ responses	Institutional type				Institution control				Number of undergraduates enrolled											Total	
	Two-year		Four-year		Public		Private		Fewer than 1,000		1,001-2,500		2,501-5,000		5,001-10,000		More than 10,000					
	Freq.	%	Freq	%	Freq.	%	Freq.	%	Freq.	%	Freq.	%	Freq.	%	Freq.	%	Freq.	%			Freq.	%
Q36. What is the approximate percentage of sophomore students reached by academic advising for sophomores on your campus?																						
91-100%	1	12.5%	41	77.4%	19	57.6%	22	84.6%	6	85.7%	12	85.7%	3	37.5%	11	84.6%	10	52.6%			42	68.9%
Total	8	100.0%	53	100.0%	33	100.0%	26	100.0%	7	100.0%	14	100.0%	8	100.0%	13	100.0%	19	100.0%			61	100.0%
Q37. What proportion of your sophomore students are required to participate in academic advising?																						
None are required to participate	4	25.0%	18	13.4%	12	15.4%	10	14.3%	2	13.3%	6	16.2%	6	21.4%	2	6.9%	6	14.6%			22	14.7%
Less than 10%	0	0.0%	1	0.7%	0	0.0%	1	1.4%	0	0.0%	1	2.7%	0	0.0%	0	0.0%	0	0.0%			1	0.7%
10-19%	0	0.0%	2	1.5%	1	1.3%	1	1.4%	0	0.0%	1	2.7%	0	0.0%	0	0.0%	1	2.4%			2	1.3%
20-29%	1	6.3%	5	3.7%	5	6.4%	1	1.4%	1	6.7%	0	0.0%	1	3.6%	0	0.0%	4	9.8%			6	4.0%
30-39%	0	0.0%	2	1.5%	2	2.6%	0	0.0%	0	0.0%	0	0.0%	1	3.6%	1	3.4%	0	0.0%			2	1.3%
40-49%	0	0.0%	5	3.7%	3	3.8%	2	2.9%	0	0.0%	0	0.0%	0	0.0%	4	13.8%	1	2.4%			5	3.3%
50-59%	0	0.0%	1	0.7%	1	1.3%	0	0.0%	0	0.0%	0	0.0%	0	0.0%	0	0.0%	1	2.4%			1	0.7%
60-69%	1	6.3%	3	2.2%	4	5.1%	0	0.0%	0	0.0%	0	0.0%	1	3.6%	0	0.0%	3	7.3%			4	2.7%
70-79%	0	0.0%	0	0.0%	0	0.0%	0	0.0%	0	0.0%	0	0.0%	0	0.0%	0	0.0%	0	0.0%			0	0.0%
80-89%	1	6.3%	2	1.5%	2	2.6%	1	1.4%	0	0.0%	1	2.7%	1	3.6%	0	0.0%	1	2.4%			3	2.0%
90-99%	0	0.0%	5	3.7%	3	3.8%	2	2.9%	0	0.0%	1	2.7%	0	0.0%	1	3.4%	3	7.3%			5	3.3%
100% - All sophomore students are required to participate	9	56.3%	90	67.2%	45	57.7%	52	74.3%	12	80.0%	27	73.0%	18	64.3%	21	72.4%	21	51.2%			99	66.0%
Total	16	100.0%	134	100.0%	78	100.0%	70	100.0%	15	100.0%	37	100.0%	28	100.0%	29	100.0%	41	100.0%			150	100.0%

Table continues on page 110

Table continued from page 109

Q38. Which of the following groups of sophomore students are required to participate in academic advising?

Survey question/ responses	Institutional type				Institution control				Number of undergraduates enrolled											Total	
	Two-year		Four-year		Public		Private		Fewer than 1,000		1,001-2,500		2,501-5,000		5,001-10,000		More than 10,000					
	Freq.	%	Freq.	%	Freq.	%	Freq.	%	Freq.	%	Freq.	%	Freq.	%	Freq.	%	Freq.	%	Freq.	%
Academically underprepared students	3	100.0%	9	34.6%	8	38.1%	4	50.0%	1	100.0%	2	50.0%	4	100.0%	1	16.7%	4	28.6%	12	41.4%
First-generation students	1	33.3%	5	19.2%	3	14.3%	3	37.5%	0	0.0%	2	50.0%	1	25.0%	1	16.7%	2	14.3%	6	20.7%
Honors students	1	33.3%	13	50.0%	10	47.6%	4	50.0%	0	0.0%	1	25.0%	2	50.0%	4	66.7%	7	50.0%	14	48.3%
International students	1	33.3%	8	30.8%	5	23.8%	4	50.0%	0	0.0%	2	50.0%	1	25.0%	3	50.0%	3	21.4%	9	31.0%
Learning community participants	0	0.0%	4	15.4%	2	9.5%	2	25.0%	0	0.0%	0	0.0%	1	25.0%	1	16.7%	2	14.3%	4	13.8%
Preprofessional students (e.g., prelaw, premed)	0	0.0%	3	11.5%	1	4.8%	2	25.0%	0	0.0%	0	0.0%	1	25.0%	1	16.7%	1	7.1%	3	10.3%
Student athletes	1	33.3%	18	69.2%	15	71.4%	4	50.0%	0	0.0%	2	50.0%	1	25.0%	5	83.3%	11	78.6%	19	65.5%
Students enrolled in developmental or remedial courses	1	33.3%	7	26.9%	6	28.6%	2	25.0%	0	0.0%	1	25.0%	3	75.0%	1	16.7%	3	21.4%	8	27.6%
Students on probationary status	3	100.0%	21	80.8%	17	81.0%	7	87.5%	1	100.0%	4	100.0%	4	100.0%	3	50.0%	12	85.7%	24	82.8%
Students residing within a particular residence hall	1	33.3%	2	7.7%	1	4.8%	2	25.0%	0	0.0%	1	25.0%	1	25.0%	1	16.7%	0	0.0%	3	10.3%
Students with fewer credits than necessary for sophomore status	0	0.0%	5	19.2%	3	14.3%	2	25.0%	0	0.0%	0	0.0%	2	50.0%	1	16.7%	2	14.3%	5	17.2%
Students within specific majors	0	0.0%	8	30.8%	6	28.6%	2	25.0%	0	0.0%	0	0.0%	0	0.0%	4	66.7%	4	28.6%	8	27.6%
TRIO participants	1	33.3%	9	34.6%	8	38.1%	2	25.0%	0	0.0%	1	25.0%	0	0.0%	4	66.7%	5	35.7%	10	34.5%

Table continues on page 111

Table continued from page 110

Survey question/responses	Institutional type				Institution control				Number of undergraduates enrolled										Total	
	Two-year		Four-year		Public		Private		Fewer than 1,000		1,001-2,500		2,501-5,000		5,001-10,000		More than 10,000			
	Freq.	%	Freq	%	Freq.	%	Freq.	%	Freq.	%	Freq.	%	Freq.	%	Freq.	%	Freq.	%	Freq.	%
Q38. Which of the following groups of sophomore students are required to participate in academic advising?																				
Undeclared students	0	0.0%	15	57.7%	11	52.4%	4	50.0%	0	0.0%	1	25.0%	3	75.0%	3	50.0%	8	57.1%	15	51.7%
Other	0	0.0%	4	15.4%	4	19.0%	0	0.0%	0	0.0%	0	0.0%	0	0.0%	0	0.0%	4	28.6%	4	13.8%
Total	3	100.0%	26	100.0%	21	100.0%	8	100.0%	1	100.0%	4	100.0%	4	100.0%	6	100.0%	14	100.0%	29	100.0%
Q39. Which of the following groups of sophomore students are specifically targeted by academic advising for sophomores?																				
All sophomore students	6	75.0%	47	88.7%	25	75.8%	26	100.0%	7	100.0%	14	100.0%	7	87.5%	10	76.9%	15	78.9%	53	86.9%
Academically underprepared students	3	37.5%	12	22.6%	9	27.3%	5	19.2%	1	14.3%	2	14.3%	2	25.0%	4	30.8%	6	31.6%	15	24.6%
First-generation students	2	25.0%	8	15.1%	6	18.2%	4	15.4%	1	14.3%	3	21.4%	0	0.0%	2	15.4%	4	21.1%	10	16.4%
Honors students	1	12.5%	9	17.0%	5	15.2%	5	19.2%	1	14.3%	2	14.3%	0	0.0%	4	30.8%	3	15.8%	10	16.4%
International students	1	12.5%	9	17.0%	5	15.2%	4	15.4%	1	14.3%	2	14.3%	1	12.5%	4	30.8%	2	10.5%	10	16.4%
Learning community participants	1	12.5%	3	5.7%	2	6.1%	2	7.7%	0	0.0%	1	7.1%	0	0.0%	2	15.4%	1	5.3%	4	6.6%
Preprofessional students (e.g., prelaw, premed)	0	0.0%	7	13.2%	2	6.1%	5	19.2%	1	14.3%	1	7.1%	1	12.5%	3	23.1%	1	5.3%	7	11.5%
Student athletes	5	62.5%	14	26.4%	14	42.4%	4	15.4%	1	14.3%	2	14.3%	2	25.0%	7	53.8%	7	36.8%	19	31.1%
Students enrolled in developmental or remedial courses	3	37.5%	3	5.7%	4	12.1%	1	3.8%	0	0.0%	1	7.1%	1	12.5%	2	15.4%	2	10.5%	6	9.8%
Students on probationary status	4	50.0%	18	34.0%	13	39.4%	8	30.8%	1	14.3%	4	28.6%	4	50.0%	6	46.2%	7	36.8%	22	36.1%

Table continues on page 112

Table continued from page 111

Q39. Which of the following groups of sophomore students are specifically targeted by academic advising for sophomores?

Survey question/ responses	Institutional type				Institution control				Number of undergraduates enrolled										Total	
	Two-year		Four-year		Public		Private		Fewer than 1,000		1,001-2,500		2,501-5,000		5,001-10,000		More than 10,000			
	Freq.	%	Freq.	%	Freq.	%	Freq.	%	Freq.	%	Freq.	%	Freq.	%	Freq.	%	Freq.	%	Freq.	%
Students residing within a particular residence hall	1	12.5%	1	1.9%	1	3.0%	1	3.8%	0	0.0%	1	7.1%	0	0.0%	1	7.7%	0	0.0%	2	3.3%
Students with fewer credits than necessary for sophomore status	0	0.0%	6	11.3%	3	9.1%	3	11.5%	0	0.0%	2	14.3%	0	0.0%	1	7.7%	3	15.8%	6	9.8%
Students within specific majors	0	0.0%	2	3.8%	1	3.0%	1	3.8%	0	0.0%	0	0.0%	0	0.0%	1	7.7%	1	5.3%	2	3.3%
TRIO participants	1	12.5%	5	9.4%	6	18.2%	0	0.0%	0	0.0%	1	7.1%	0	0.0%	3	23.1%	2	10.5%	6	9.8%
Undeclared students	0	0.0%	13	24.5%	6	18.2%	7	26.9%	2	28.6%	1	7.1%	2	25.0%	4	30.8%	4	21.1%	13	21.3%
Other	0	0.0%	0	0.0%	0	0.0%	0	0.0%	0	0.0%	0	0.0%	0	0.0%	0	0.0%	0	0.0%	0	0.0%
No sophomore students are specifically targeted by academic advising	0	0.0%	2	3.8%	2	6.1%	0	0.0%	0	0.0%	0	0.0%	0	0.0%	1	7.7%	1	5.3%	2	3.3%
Total	8	100.0%	53	100.0%	33	100.0%	26	100.0%	7	100.0%	14	100.0%	8	100.0%	13	100.0%	19	100.0%	61	100.0%

Q40. How long has academic advising for sophomores been in place?

Survey question/ responses	Two-year		Four-year		Public		Private		Fewer than 1,000		1,001-2,500		2,501-5,000		5,001-10,000		More than 10,000		Total	
	Freq.	%	Freq.	%	Freq.	%	Freq.	%	Freq.	%	Freq.	%	Freq.	%	Freq.	%	Freq.	%	Freq.	%
2 years or less	0	0.0%	4	7.5%	1	3.0%	3	11.5%	0	0.0%	1	7.1%	2	25.0%	0	0.0%	1	5.3%	4	6.6%
3-5 years	3	37.5%	7	13.2%	7	21.2%	3	11.5%	1	14.3%	3	21.4%	1	12.5%	2	15.4%	3	15.8%	10	16.4%
6-10 years	2	25.0%	9	17.0%	8	24.2%	3	11.5%	1	14.3%	1	7.1%	1	12.5%	1	7.7%	7	36.8%	11	18.0%
11-15 years	0	0.0%	6	11.3%	5	15.2%	1	3.8%	0	0.0%	1	7.1%	1	12.5%	2	15.4%	2	10.5%	6	9.8%
16-20 years	0	0.0%	4	7.5%	2	6.1%	1	3.8%	0	0.0%	0	0.0%	1	12.5%	1	7.7%	2	10.5%	4	6.6%
More than 20 years	3	37.5%	23	43.4%	10	30.3%	15	57.7%	5	71.4%	8	57.1%	2	25.0%	7	53.8%	4	21.1%	26	42.6%
Total	8	100.0%	53	100.0%	33	100.0%	26	100.0%	7	100.0%	14	100.0%	8	100.0%	13	100.0%	19	100.0%	61	100.0%

Table continues on page 113

Table continued from page 112

Q41. Please select the three most important objectives for academic advising in the sophomore year.

Survey question/ responses	Institutional type				Institution control				Number of undergraduates enrolled										Total	
	Two-year		Four-year		Public		Private		Fewer than 1,000		1,001-2,500		2,501-5,000		5,001-10,000		More than 10,000			
	Freq.	%	Freq.	%	Freq.	%	Freq.	%	Freq.	%	Freq.	%	Freq.	%	Freq.	%	Freq.	%	Freq.	%
Academic planning	7	87.5%	47	88.7%	31	93.9%	23	88.5%	5	71.4%	12	85.7%	7	87.5%	12	92.3%	18	94.7%	54	88.5%
Academic success strategies	1	12.5%	18	34.0%	12	36.4%	6	23.1%	1	14.3%	2	14.3%	4	50.0%	5	38.5%	7	36.8%	19	31.1%
Analytical, critical-thinking, or problem-solving skills	2	25.0%	2	3.8%	3	9.1%	0	0.0%	1	14.3%	1	7.1%	0	0.0%	2	15.4%	0	0.0%	4	6.6%
Career exploration and/or preparation	3	37.5%	17	32.1%	9	27.3%	11	42.3%	1	14.3%	5	35.7%	4	50.0%	2	15.4%	8	42.1%	20	32.8%
Civic engagement	0	0.0%	0	0.0%	0	0.0%	0	0.0%	0	0.0%	0	0.0%	0	0.0%	0	0.0%	0	0.0%	0	0.0%
Common sophomore-year experience	0	0.0%	0	0.0%	0	0.0%	0	0.0%	0	0.0%	0	0.0%	0	0.0%	0	0.0%	0	0.0%	0	0.0%
Connection with the institution or campus	1	12.5%	2	3.8%	2	6.1%	1	3.8%	0	0.0%	1	7.1%	0	0.0%	0	0.0%	2	10.5%	3	4.9%
Developmental education, remediation, and/or review	0	0.0%	0	0.0%	0	0.0%	0	0.0%	0	0.0%	0	0.0%	0	0.0%	0	0.0%	0	0.0%	0	0.0%
Digital literacy	0	0.0%	0	0.0%	0	0.0%	0	0.0%	0	0.0%	0	0.0%	0	0.0%	0	0.0%	0	0.0%	0	0.0%
Discipline-specific knowledge	1	12.5%	9	17.0%	4	12.1%	6	23.1%	2	28.6%	2	14.3%	2	25.0%	2	15.4%	2	10.5%	10	16.4%
Graduate or professional school preparation (e.g., premed, prelaw)	0	0.0%	0	0.0%	0	0.0%	0	0.0%	0	0.0%	0	0.0%	0	0.0%	0	0.0%	0	0.0%	0	0.0%
Health and wellness	0	0.0%	1	1.9%	0	0.0%	1	3.8%	0	0.0%	1	7.1%	0	0.0%	0	0.0%	0	0.0%	1	1.6%
Information literacy	1	12.5%	0	0.0%	1	3.0%	0	0.0%	0	0.0%	0	0.0%	0	0.0%	0	0.0%	1	5.3%	1	1.6%

Table continues on page 114

Table continued from page 113

Q41. Please select the three most important objectives for academic advising in the sophomore year.

Survey question/ responses	Institutional type				Institution control				Number of undergraduates enrolled										Total	
	Two-year		Four-year		Public		Private		Fewer than 1,000		1,001-2,500		2,501-5,000		5,001-10,000		More than 10,000			
	Freq.	%	Freq.	%	Freq.	%	Freq.	%	Freq.	%	Freq.	%	Freq.	%	Freq.	%	Freq.	%	Freq.	%
Integrative and applied learning	0	0.0%	0	0.0%	0	0.0%	0	0.0%	0	0.0%	0	0.0%	0	0.0%	0	0.0%	0	0.0%	0	0.0%
Intercultural competence, diversity skills, or engaging with different perspectives	0	0.0%	0	0.0%	0	0.0%	0	0.0%	0	0.0%	0	0.0%	0	0.0%	0	0.0%	0	0.0%	0	0.0%
Introduction to a major, discipline, or career path	1	12.5%	15	28.3%	9	27.3%	7	26.9%	2	28.6%	2	14.3%	0	0.0%	8	61.5%	4	21.1%	16	26.2%
Introduction to college-level academic expectations	0	0.0%	2	3.8%	2	6.1%	0	0.0%	0	0.0%	0	0.0%	0	0.0%	0	0.0%	2	10.5%	2	3.3%
Introduction to the liberal arts	0	0.0%	0	0.0%	0	0.0%	0	0.0%	0	0.0%	0	0.0%	0	0.0%	0	0.0%	0	0.0%	0	0.0%
Knowledge of institution or campus resources and services	0	0.0%	8	15.1%	5	15.2%	1	3.8%	1	14.3%	0	0.0%	2	25.0%	2	15.4%	3	15.8%	8	13.1%
Major exploration	2	25.0%	16	30.2%	8	24.2%	10	38.5%	4	57.1%	3	21.4%	1	12.5%	6	46.2%	4	21.1%	18	29.5%
Oral communication skills	0	0.0%	0	0.0%	0	0.0%	0	0.0%	0	0.0%	0	0.0%	0	0.0%	0	0.0%	0	0.0%	0	0.0%
Persistence, retention, or third-year return rates	0	0.0%	11	20.8%	5	15.2%	5	19.2%	0	0.0%	5	35.7%	1	12.5%	0	0.0%	5	26.3%	11	18.0%
Personal exploration or development	0	0.0%	3	5.7%	1	3.0%	2	7.7%	0	0.0%	2	14.3%	0	0.0%	0	0.0%	1	5.3%	3	4.9%

Table continues on page 115

Table continued from page 114

Survey question/ responses	Institutional type				Institution control				Number of undergraduates enrolled										Total	
	Two-year		Four-year		Public		Private		Fewer than 1,000		1,001-2,500		2,501-5,000		5,001-10,000		More than 10,000			
	Freq.	%	Freq.	%	Freq.	%	Freq.	%	Freq.	%	Freq.	%	Freq.	%	Freq.	%	Freq.	%	Freq.	%
Q41. Please select the three most important objectives for academic advising in the sophomore year.																				
Project planning, teamwork, or management skills	1	12.5%	0	0.0%	1	3.0%	0	0.0%	0	0.0%	1	7.1%	0	0.0%	0	0.0%	0	0.0%	1	1.6%
Social support networks (e.g., friendships)	0	0.0%	0	0.0%	0	0.0%	0	0.0%	0	0.0%	0	0.0%	0	0.0%	0	0.0%	0	0.0%	0	0.0%
Student-faculty interaction	0	0.0%	5	9.4%	1	3.0%	4	15.4%	2	28.6%	1	7.1%	2	25.0%	0	0.0%	0	0.0%	5	8.2%
Writing skills	0	0.0%	1	1.9%	0	0.0%	0	0.0%	1	14.3%	0	0.0%	0	0.0%	0	0.0%	0	0.0%	1	1.6%
Other	2	25.0%	1	1.9%	2	6.1%	1	3.8%	1	14.3%	1	7.1%	1	12.5%	0	0.0%	0	0.0%	3	4.9%
Total	8	100.0%	53	100.0%	33	100.0%	26	100.0%	7	100.0%	14	100.0%	8	100.0%	13	100.0%	19	100.0%	61	100.0%
Q42. To what extent are each of the following elements present in academic advising for sophomores? - Performance expectations set at appropriately high levels																				
Element is not present - 1	0	0.0%	7	13.5%	4	12.5%	3	12.0%	0	0.0%	2	15.4%	2	25.0%	0	0.0%	3	16.7%	7	11.9%
2	0	0.0%	3	5.8%	2	6.3%	1	4.0%	0	0.0%	1	7.7%	0	0.0%	1	7.7%	1	5.6%	3	5.1%
Element is partially present - 3	3	42.9%	21	40.4%	13	40.6%	11	44.0%	2	28.6%	5	38.5%	2	25.0%	7	53.8%	8	44.4%	24	40.7%
4	3	42.9%	13	25.0%	10	31.3%	6	24.0%	3	42.9%	2	15.4%	3	37.5%	3	23.1%	5	27.8%	16	27.1%
Element is pervasive throughout initiative - 5	1	14.3%	8	15.4%	3	9.4%	4	16.0%	2	28.6%	3	23.1%	1	12.5%	2	15.4%	1	5.6%	9	15.3%
Total	7	100.0%	52	100.0%	32	100.0%	25	100.0%	7	100.0%	13	100.0%	8	100.0%	13	100.0%	18	100.0%	59	100.0%
Q43. To what extent are each of the following elements present in academic advising for sophomores? - Significant investment of time and effort by students over an extended period of time																				
Element is not present - 1	0	0.0%	7	13.5%	5	15.6%	2	8.0%	0	0.0%	2	15.4%	0	0.0%	1	7.7%	4	22.2%	7	11.9%
2	0	0.0%	7	13.5%	3	9.4%	4	16.0%	0	0.0%	2	15.4%	1	12.5%	2	15.4%	2	11.1%	7	11.9%

Table continues on page 116

Table continued from page 115

Survey question/ responses	Institutional type				Institution control				Number of undergraduates enrolled										Total	
	Two-year		Four-year		Public		Private		Fewer than 1,000		1,001-2,500		2,501-5,000		5,001-10,000		More than 10,000			
	Freq.	%	Freq.	%	Freq.	%	Freq.	%	Freq.	%	Freq.	%	Freq.	%	Freq.	%	Freq.	%	Freq.	%
Q43. To what extent are each of the following elements present in academic advising for sophomores? - Significant investment of time and effort by students over an extended period of time																				
Element is partially present - 3	5	71.4%	23	44.2%	16	50.0%	12	48.0%	2	28.6%	5	38.5%	5	62.5%	7	53.8%	9	50.0%	28	47.5%
4	2	28.6%	8	15.4%	5	15.6%	5	20.0%	2	28.6%	3	23.1%	1	12.5%	1	7.7%	3	16.7%	10	16.9%
Element is pervasive throughout initiative - 5	0	0.0%	7	13.5%	3	9.4%	2	8.0%	3	42.9%	1	7.7%	1	12.5%	2	15.4%	0	0.0%	7	11.9%
Total	7	100.0%	52	100.0%	32	100.0%	25	100.0%	7	100.0%	13	100.0%	8	100.0%	13	100.0%	18	100.0%	59	100.0%
Q44. To what extent are each of the following elements present in academic advising for sophomores? - Interactions with faculty and peers about substantive matters																				
Element is not present - 1	0	0.0%	2	3.8%	2	6.3%	0	0.0%	0	0.0%	0	0.0%	0	0.0%	0	0.0%	2	11.1%	2	3.4%
2	2	28.6%	7	13.5%	6	18.8%	3	12.0%	1	14.3%	2	15.4%	0	0.0%	3	23.1%	3	16.7%	9	15.3%
Element is partially present - 3	1	14.3%	24	46.2%	12	37.5%	13	52.0%	2	28.6%	6	46.2%	3	37.5%	7	53.8%	7	38.9%	25	42.4%
4	3	42.9%	9	17.3%	8	25.0%	4	16.0%	1	14.3%	2	15.4%	3	37.5%	2	15.4%	4	22.2%	12	20.3%
Element is pervasive throughout initiative - 5	1	14.3%	10	19.2%	4	12.5%	5	20.0%	3	42.9%	3	23.1%	2	25.0%	1	7.7%	2	11.1%	11	18.6%
Total	7	100.0%	52	100.0%	32	100.0%	25	100.0%	7	100.0%	13	100.0%	8	100.0%	13	100.0%	18	100.0%	59	100.0%
Q45. To what extent are each of the following elements present in academic advising for sophomores? - Experiences with diversity, wherein students are exposed to and must contend with people and circumstances that differ from those with which students are familiar																				
Element is not present - 1	2	28.6%	12	23.1%	8	25.0%	6	24.0%	0	0.0%	3	23.1%	3	37.5%	3	23.1%	5	27.8%	14	23.7%
2	0	0.0%	11	21.2%	7	21.9%	4	16.0%	0	0.0%	3	23.1%	0	0.0%	4	30.8%	4	22.2%	11	18.6%
Element is partially present - 3	4	57.1%	17	32.7%	11	34.4%	10	40.0%	2	28.6%	7	53.8%	2	25.0%	5	38.5%	5	27.8%	21	35.6%

Table continues on page 117

Table continued from page 116

Survey question/ responses	Institutional type				Institution control				Number of undergraduates enrolled											
	Two-year		Four-year		Public		Private		Fewer than 1,000		1,001-2,500		2,501-5,000		5,001-10,000		More than 10,000		Total	
	Freq.	%	Freq.	%	Freq.	%	Freq.	%	Freq.	%	Freq.	%	Freq.	%	Freq.	%	Freq.	%	Freq.	%
Q45. To what extent are each of the following elements present in academic advising for sophomores? - Experiences with diversity, wherein students are exposed to and must contend with people and circumstances that differ from those with which students are familiar																				
4	0	0.0%	6	11.5%	2	6.3%	4	16.0%	3	42.9%	0	0.0%	1	12.5%	0	0.0%	2	11.1%	6	10.2%
Element is pervasive throughout initiative - 5	1	14.3%	6	11.5%	4	12.5%	1	4.0%	2	28.6%	0	0.0%	2	25.0%	1	7.7%	2	11.1%	7	11.9%
Total	7	100.0%	52	100.0%	32	100.0%	25	100.0%	7	100.0%	13	100.0%	8	100.0%	13	100.0%	18	100.0%	59	100.0%
Q46. To what extent are each of the following elements present in academic advising for sophomores? - Frequent, timely, and constructive feedback																				
Element is not present - 1	1	14.3%	5	9.6%	5	15.6%	1	4.0%	0	0.0%	2	15.4%	0	0.0%	2	15.4%	2	11.1%	6	10.2%
2	0	0.0%	7	13.5%	3	9.4%	4	16.0%	0	0.0%	1	7.7%	2	25.0%	2	15.4%	2	11.1%	7	11.9%
Element is partially present - 3	3	42.9%	19	36.5%	12	37.5%	10	40.0%	3	42.9%	4	30.8%	2	25.0%	6	46.2%	7	38.9%	22	37.3%
4	2	28.6%	10	19.2%	8	25.0%	4	16.0%	2	28.6%	1	7.7%	3	37.5%	1	7.7%	5	27.8%	12	20.3%
Element is pervasive throughout initiative - 5	1	14.3%	11	21.2%	4	12.5%	6	24.0%	2	28.6%	5	38.5%	1	12.5%	2	15.4%	2	11.1%	12	20.3%
Total	7	100.0%	52	100.0%	32	100.0%	25	100.0%	7	100.0%	13	100.0%	8	100.0%	13	100.0%	18	100.0%	59	100.0%
Q47. To what extent are each of the following elements present in academic advising for sophomores? - Periodic, structured opportunities to reflect and integrate learning																				
Element is not present - 1	0	0.0%	11	21.2%	6	18.8%	5	20.0%	0	0.0%	3	23.1%	2	25.0%	2	15.4%	4	22.2%	11	18.6%
2	1	14.3%	7	13.5%	6	18.8%	2	8.0%	0	0.0%	0	0.0%	2	25.0%	3	23.1%	3	16.7%	8	13.6%
Element is partially present - 3	3	42.9%	20	38.5%	13	40.6%	10	40.0%	3	42.9%	6	46.2%	1	12.5%	7	53.8%	6	33.3%	23	39.0%
4	3	42.9%	9	17.3%	6	18.8%	6	24.0%	2	28.6%	3	23.1%	2	25.0%	0	0.0%	5	27.8%	12	20.3%

Table continues on page 118

Table continued from page 117

| | Institutional type | | | | Institution control | | | | Number of undergraduates enrolled | | | | | | | | | | Total | |
| | Two-year | | Four-year | | Public | | Private | | Fewer than 1,000 | | 1,001-2,500 | | 2,501-5,000 | | 5,001-10,000 | | More than 10,000 | | | |
Survey question/responses	Freq.	%	Freq	%	Freq.	%	Freq.	%	Freq.	%	Freq.	%	Freq.	%	Freq.	%	Freq.	%	Freq.	%
Q47. To what extent are each of the following elements present in academic advising for sophomores? - Periodic, structured opportunities to reflect and integrate learning																				
Element is pervasive throughout initiative -5	0	0.0%	5	9.6%	1	3.1%	2	8.0%	2	28.6%	1	7.7%	1	12.5%	1	7.7%	0	0.0%	5	8.5%
Total	7	100.0%	52	100.0%	32	100.0%	25	100.0%	7	100.0%	13	100.0%	8	100.0%	13	100.0%	18	100.0%	59	100.0%
Q48. To what extent are each of the following elements present in academic advising for sophomores? - Opportunities to discover relevance of learning through real-world applications																				
Element is not present - 1	1	14.3%	12	23.1%	7	21.9%	6	24.0%	1	14.3%	4	30.8%	1	12.5%	2	15.4%	5	27.8%	13	22.0%
2	0	0.0%	6	11.5%	2	6.3%	4	16.0%	1	14.3%	1	7.7%	1	12.5%	2	15.4%	1	5.6%	6	10.2%
Element is partially present - 3	4	57.1%	17	32.7%	15	46.9%	6	24.0%	0	0.0%	3	23.1%	3	37.5%	8	61.5%	7	38.9%	21	35.6%
4	1	14.3%	13	25.0%	5	15.6%	9	36.0%	4	57.1%	5	38.5%	2	25.0%	0	0.0%	3	16.7%	14	23.7%
Element is pervasive throughout initiative -5	1	14.3%	4	7.7%	3	9.4%	0	0.0%	1	14.3%	0	0.0%	1	12.5%	1	7.7%	2	11.1%	5	8.5%
Total	7	100.0%	52	100.0%	32	100.0%	25	100.0%	7	100.0%	13	100.0%	8	100.0%	13	100.0%	18	100.0%	59	100.0%
Q49. To what extent are each of the following elements present in academic advising for sophomores? - Public demonstration of competence																				
Element is not present - 1	2	28.6%	16	30.8%	10	31.3%	8	32.0%	1	14.3%	5	38.5%	2	25.0%	4	30.8%	6	33.3%	18	30.5%
2	0	0.0%	13	25.0%	5	15.6%	8	32.0%	2	28.6%	3	23.1%	2	25.0%	2	15.4%	4	22.2%	13	22.0%
Element is partially present - 3	4	57.1%	13	25.0%	11	34.4%	6	24.0%	1	14.3%	5	38.5%	1	12.5%	4	30.8%	6	33.3%	17	28.8%
4	0	0.0%	5	9.6%	3	9.4%	2	8.0%	0	0.0%	0	0.0%	2	25.0%	2	15.4%	1	5.6%	5	8.5%
Element is pervasive throughout initiative -5	1	14.3%	5	9.6%	3	9.4%	1	4.0%	3	42.9%	0	0.0%	1	12.5%	1	7.7%	1	5.6%	6	10.2%
Total	7	100.0%	52	100.0%	32	100.0%	25	100.0%	7	100.0%	13	100.0%	8	100.0%	13	100.0%	18	100.0%	59	100.0%

Table continues on page 119

Table continued from page 118

Survey question/ responses	Institutional type				Institution control				Number of undergraduates enrolled										Total	
	Two-year		Four-year		Public		Private		Fewer than 1,000		1,001-2,500		2,501-5,000		5,001-10,000		More than 10,000			
	Freq.	%	Freq.	%	Freq.	%	Freq.	%	Freq.	%	Freq.	%	Freq.	%	Freq.	%	Freq.	%	Freq.	%
Q50. Which campus unit directly administers academic advising for sophomores?																				
Academic affairs central office	3	20.0%	34	25.6%	10	13.0%	27	39.1%	7	46.7%	12	33.3%	10	35.7%	6	20.7%	2	5.0%	37	25.0%
Academic department(s) (please list)	2	13.3%	26	19.5%	12	15.6%	15	21.7%	4	26.7%	11	30.6%	3	10.7%	5	17.2%	5	12.5%	28	18.9%
College or school (e.g., College of Liberal Arts)	0	0.0%	37	27.8%	25	32.5%	12	17.4%	1	6.7%	4	11.1%	1	3.6%	9	31.0%	22	55.0%	37	25.0%
Sophomore-year program office	1	6.7%	1	0.8%	1	1.3%	1	1.4%	0	0.0%	1	2.8%	0	0.0%	1	3.4%	0	0.0%	2	1.4%
Student affairs central office	5	33.3%	4	3.0%	8	10.4%	0	0.0%	2	13.3%	1	2.8%	3	10.7%	0	0.0%	3	7.5%	9	6.1%
University college	0	0.0%	5	3.8%	3	3.9%	2	2.9%	0	0.0%	1	2.8%	1	3.6%	2	6.9%	1	2.5%	5	3.4%
Other, please specify.	4	26.7%	26	19.5%	18	23.4%	12	17.4%	1	6.7%	6	16.7%	10	35.7%	6	20.7%	7	17.5%	30	20.3%
Total	15	100.0%	133	100.0%	77	100.0%	69	100.0%	15	100.0%	36	100.0%	28	100.0%	29	100.0%	40	100.0%	148	100.0%
Q51. How is academic advising for sophomores primarily funded?																				
Auxillary funds	0	0.0%	0	0.0%	0	0.0%	0	0.0%	0	0.0%	0	0.0%	0	0.0%	0	0.0%	0	0.0%	0	0.0%
Foundation funds	0	0.0%	0	0.0%	0	0.0%	0	0.0%	0	0.0%	0	0.0%	0	0.0%	0	0.0%	0	0.0%	0	0.0%
Grant funds	1	6.7%	4	3.0%	3	3.9%	2	2.9%	0	0.0%	2	5.6%	0	0.0%	2	6.9%	1	2.5%	5	3.4%
Nonrecurring or one-time funds	1	6.7%	1	0.8%	2	2.6%	0	0.0%	0	0.0%	0	0.0%	0	0.0%	1	3.4%	1	2.5%	2	1.4%
Recurring state- or university-appropriated funds	6	40.0%	43	32.3%	35	45.5%	14	20.3%	3	20.0%	9	25.0%	11	39.3%	9	31.0%	17	42.5%	49	33.1%
Student activity fees	0	0.0%	4	3.0%	4	5.2%	0	0.0%	0	0.0%	0	0.0%	0	0.0%	2	6.9%	2	5.0%	4	2.7%

Table continues on page 120

Table continued from page 119

Survey question/responses	Institutional type				Institution control				Number of undergraduates enrolled										Total	
	Two-year		Four-year		Public		Private		Fewer than 1,000		1,001-2,500		2,501-5,000		5,001-10,000		More than 10,000			
	Freq.	%	Freq	%	Freq.	%	Freq.	%	Freq.	%	Freq.	%	Freq.	%	Freq.	%	Freq.	%	Freq.	%
Q51. How is academic advising for sophomores primarily funded?																				
Tuition revenue	5	33.3%	64	48.1%	24	31.2%	43	62.3%	10	66.7%	20	55.6%	14	50.0%	11	37.9%	14	35.0%	69	46.6%
Other, please specify.	2	13.3%	17	12.8%	9	11.7%	10	14.5%	2	13.3%	5	13.9%	3	10.7%	4	13.8%	5	12.5%	19	12.8%
Total	15	100.0%	133	100.0%	77	100.0%	69	100.0%	15	100.0%	36	100.0%	28	100.0%	29	100.0%	40	100.0%	148	100.0%
Q52. Please identify the activities and processes related to academic advising in which your institution is currently engaged (Select all that apply)																				
Campuswide assessment and planning	11	73.3%	65	48.9%	45	58.4%	31	44.9%	8	53.3%	21	58.3%	14	50.0%	10	34.5%	23	57.5%	76	51.4%
Evaluation and continuous improvement of advising	13	86.7%	106	79.7%	65	84.4%	53	76.8%	12	80.0%	28	77.8%	23	82.1%	21	72.4%	35	87.5%	119	80.4%
Leadership and change management	2	13.3%	33	24.8%	24	31.2%	11	15.9%	4	26.7%	5	13.9%	5	17.9%	6	20.7%	15	37.5%	35	23.6%
Ongoing professional development and training for advisors	10	66.7%	101	75.9%	60	77.9%	51	73.9%	10	66.7%	23	63.9%	20	71.4%	21	72.4%	37	92.5%	111	75.0%
Process mapping	3	20.0%	29	21.8%	21	27.3%	11	15.9%	2	13.3%	8	22.2%	3	10.7%	5	17.2%	14	35.0%	32	21.6%
Structure redesign	4	26.7%	35	26.3%	19	24.7%	20	29.0%	2	13.3%	12	33.3%	10	35.7%	8	27.6%	7	17.5%	39	26.4%
Technology and data governance and management	4	26.7%	47	35.3%	31	40.3%	20	29.0%	3	20.0%	10	27.8%	11	39.3%	10	34.5%	17	42.5%	51	34.5%
Technology selection	3	20.0%	32	24.1%	22	28.6%	13	18.8%	3	20.0%	6	16.7%	5	17.9%	6	20.7%	15	37.5%	35	23.6%
Other	0	0.0%	14	10.5%	10	13.0%	3	4.3%	1	6.7%	1	2.8%	0	0.0%	7	24.1%	5	12.5%	14	9.5%
Total	15	100.0%	133	100.0%	77	100.0%	69	100.0%	15	100.0%	36	100.0%	28	100.0%	29	100.0%	40	100.0%	148	100.0%

Table continues on page 121

Table continued from page 120

Q54. In which of the following activities and processes related to academic advising is your institution engaged in external coaching, consultation, and training? (Select all that apply)

Survey question/ responses	Institutional type				Institution control				Number of undergraduates enrolled										Total	
	Two-year		Four-year		Public		Private		Fewer than 1,000		1,001-2,500		2,501-5,000		5,001-10,000		More than 10,000			
	Freq.	%	Freq	%	Freq.	%	Freq.	%	Freq.	%	Freq.	%	Freq.	%	Freq.	%	Freq.	%	Freq.	%
Campuswide assessment and planning	4	26.7%	32	24.2%	19	24.7%	16	23.5%	5	33.3%	9	25.0%	7	25.9%	5	17.2%	10	25.0%	36	24.5%
Evaluation and continuous improvement of advising	5	33.3%	35	26.5%	25	32.5%	15	22.1%	5	33.3%	4	11.1%	8	29.6%	12	41.4%	11	27.5%	40	27.2%
Leadership and change management	3	20.0%	10	7.6%	8	10.4%	5	7.4%	0	0.0%	1	2.8%	3	11.1%	4	13.8%	5	12.5%	13	8.8%
Ongoing professional development and training for advisors	9	60.0%	50	37.9%	35	45.5%	24	35.3%	5	33.3%	14	38.9%	9	33.3%	15	51.7%	16	40.0%	59	40.1%
Process mapping	2	13.3%	4	3.0%	5	6.5%	1	1.5%	0	0.0%	1	2.8%	1	3.7%	2	6.9%	2	5.0%	6	4.1%
Structure redesign	4	26.7%	11	8.3%	11	14.3%	4	5.9%	0	0.0%	2	5.6%	5	18.5%	5	17.2%	3	7.5%	15	10.2%
Technology and data governance and management	2	13.3%	22	16.7%	15	19.5%	9	13.2%	1	6.7%	3	8.3%	5	18.5%	6	20.7%	9	22.5%	24	16.3%
Technology selection	4	26.7%	21	15.9%	16	20.8%	9	13.2%	0	0.0%	4	11.1%	6	22.2%	7	24.1%	8	20.0%	25	17.0%
Other	0	0.0%	41	31.1%	19	24.7%	21	30.9%	7	46.7%	8	22.2%	6	22.2%	10	34.5%	10	25.0%	41	27.9%
Total	15	100.0%	132	100.0%	77	100.0%	68	100.0%	15	100.0%	36	100.0%	27	100.0%	29	100.0%	40	100.0%	147	100.0%
Q55. Has academic advising for sophomores been formally assessed or evaluated in the past three years?																				
Yes	6	40.0%	36	27.3%	20	26.0%	20	29.4%	5	33.3%	11	30.6%	10	37.0%	6	20.7%	10	25.0%	42	28.6%
No	7	46.7%	68	51.5%	37	48.1%	38	55.9%	6	40.0%	21	58.3%	15	55.6%	15	51.7%	18	45.0%	75	51.0%
I don't know	2	13.3%	28	21.2%	20	26.0%	10	14.7%	4	26.7%	4	11.1%	2	7.4%	8	27.6%	12	30.0%	30	20.4%
Total	15	100.0%	132	100.0%	77	100.0%	68	100.0%	15	100.0%	36	100.0%	27	100.0%	29	100.0%	40	100.0%	147	100.0%

Table continues on page 122

Table continued from page 121

Q56: What type of assessment was conducted? (Select all that apply)

Survey question/ responses	Institutional type				Institution control				Number of undergraduates enrolled										Total	
	Two-year		Four-year		Public		Private		Fewer than 1,000		1,001-2,500		2,501-5,000		5,001-10,000		More than 10,000			
	Freq.	%	Freq.	%	Freq.	%	Freq.	%	Freq.	%	Freq.	%	Freq.	%	Freq.	%	Freq.	%	Freq.	%
Analysis of institutional data (e.g., GPA, retention rates, graduation)	5	83.3%	28	77.8%	17	85.0%	14	70.0%	5	100.0%	6	54.5%	9	90.0%	5	83.3%	8	80.0%	33	78.6%
Direct assessment of student learning outcomes	4	66.7%	11	30.6%	8	40.0%	6	30.0%	3	60.0%	1	9.1%	4	40.0%	4	66.7%	3	30.0%	15	35.7%
Focus groups with faculty	1	16.7%	10	27.8%	2	10.0%	8	40.0%	3	60.0%	5	45.5%	2	20.0%	1	16.7%	0	0.0%	11	26.2%
Focus groups with professional staff	1	16.7%	6	16.7%	2	10.0%	5	25.0%	1	20.0%	3	27.3%	2	20.0%	1	16.7%	0	0.0%	7	16.7%
Focus groups with students	2	33.3%	7	19.4%	3	15.0%	6	30.0%	1	20.0%	4	36.4%	3	30.0%	1	16.7%	0	0.0%	9	21.4%
Individual interviews with faculty	1	16.7%	5	13.9%	3	15.0%	2	10.0%	2	40.0%	1	9.1%	1	10.0%	1	16.7%	1	10.0%	6	14.3%
Individual interviews with orientation staff	1	16.7%	4	11.1%	3	15.0%	2	10.0%	0	0.0%	1	9.1%	2	20.0%	1	16.7%	1	10.0%	5	11.9%
Individual interviews with students	0	0.0%	6	16.7%	4	20.0%	1	5.0%	1	20.0%	0	0.0%	3	30.0%	1	16.7%	1	10.0%	6	14.3%
Program review	3	50.0%	7	19.4%	6	30.0%	4	20.0%	1	20.0%	1	9.1%	4	40.0%	3	50.0%	1	10.0%	10	23.8%
Student course evaluation	1	16.7%	8	22.2%	3	15.0%	5	25.0%	3	60.0%	1	9.1%	2	20.0%	3	50.0%	0	0.0%	9	21.4%
Survey instrument - Locally designed	3	50.0%	18	50.0%	11	55.0%	9	45.0%	1	20.0%	6	54.5%	4	40.0%	2	33.3%	8	80.0%	21	50.0%
Survey instrument - Nationally available	4	66.7%	7	19.4%	5	25.0%	6	30.0%	1	20.0%	4	36.4%	5	50.0%	1	16.7%	0	0.0%	11	26.2%
Other, please specify	0	0.0%	3	8.3%	0	0.0%	3	15.0%	0	0.0%	1	9.1%	1	10.0%	1	16.7%	0	0.0%	3	7.1%
Total	6	100.0%	36	100.0%	20	100.0%	20	100.0%	5	100.0%	11	100.0%	10	100.0%	6	100.0%	10	100.0%	42	100.0%

Table continues on page 123

Table continued from page 122

Survey question/ responses	Institutional type				Institution control				Number of undergraduates enrolled										Total	
	Two-year		Four-year		Public		Private		Fewer than 1,000		1,001-2,500		2,501-5,000		5,001-10,000		More than 10,000			
	Freq.	%	Freq.	%	Freq.	%	Freq.	%	Freq.	%	Freq.	%	Freq.	%	Freq.	%	Freq.	%	Freq.	%
Q57: Please identify the student learning outcomes you assessed (Select all that apply)																				
Academic planning	3	75.0%	5	45.5%	5	62.5%	3	50.0%	0	0.0%	1	100.0%	2	50.0%	3	75.0%	2	66.7%	8	53.3%
Academic success strategies	1	25.0%	9	81.8%	5	62.5%	4	66.7%	2	66.7%	0	0.0%	3	75.0%	3	75.0%	2	66.7%	10	66.7%
Analytical, critical-thinking, or problem-solving skills	2	50.0%	6	54.5%	3	37.5%	4	66.7%	3	100.0%	1	100.0%	3	75.0%	1	25.0%	0	0.0%	8	53.3%
Career exploration and/or preparation	2	50.0%	7	63.6%	6	75.0%	3	50.0%	1	33.3%	0	0.0%	3	75.0%	3	75.0%	2	66.7%	9	60.0%
Civic engagement	0	0.0%	3	27.3%	0	0.0%	3	50.0%	1	33.3%	0	0.0%	2	50.0%	0	0.0%	0	0.0%	3	20.0%
Common sophomore-year experience	0	0.0%	2	18.2%	1	12.5%	1	16.7%	0	0.0%	0	0.0%	1	25.0%	1	25.0%	0	0.0%	2	13.3%
Connection with the institution or campus	2	50.0%	5	45.5%	3	37.5%	4	66.7%	2	66.7%	0	0.0%	3	75.0%	1	25.0%	1	33.3%	7	46.7%
Developmental education, remediation, and/or review	0	0.0%	4	36.4%	1	12.5%	3	50.0%	1	33.3%	0	0.0%	1	25.0%	1	25.0%	1	33.3%	4	26.7%
Digital literacy	0	0.0%	2	18.2%	1	12.5%	1	16.7%	0	0.0%	0	0.0%	1	25.0%	1	25.0%	0	0.0%	2	13.3%
Discipline-specific knowledge	1	25.0%	2	18.2%	1	12.5%	2	33.3%	1	33.3%	0	0.0%	2	50.0%	0	0.0%	0	0.0%	3	20.0%
Graduate or professional school preparation (e.g., premed, prelaw)	0	0.0%	1	9.1%	0	0.0%	1	16.7%	0	0.0%	0	0.0%	1	25.0%	0	0.0%	0	0.0%	1	6.7%
Health and wellness	0	0.0%	2	18.2%	0	0.0%	2	33.3%	1	33.3%	0	0.0%	1	25.0%	0	0.0%	0	0.0%	2	13.3%
Information literacy	0	0.0%	2	18.2%	1	12.5%	1	16.7%	0	0.0%	0	0.0%	1	25.0%	1	25.0%	0	0.0%	2	13.3%

Table continues on page 124

Table continued from page 123

Q57: Please identify the student learning outcomes you assessed (Select all that apply)

Survey question/responses	Institutional type				Institution control				Number of undergraduates enrolled										Total	
	Two-year		Four-year		Public		Private		Fewer than 1,000		1,001-2,500		2,501-5,000		5,001-10,000		More than 10,000			
	Freq.	%	Freq.	%	Freq.	%	Freq.	%	Freq.	%	Freq.	%	Freq.	%	Freq.	%	Freq.	%	Freq.	%
Integrative and applied learning	1	25.0%	3	27.3%	2	25.0%	2	33.3%	1	33.3%	1	100.0%	1	25.0%	1	25.0%	0	0.0%	4	26.7%
Intercultural competence, diversity skills, or engaging with different perspectives	0	0.0%	4	36.4%	1	12.5%	3	50.0%	2	66.7%	0	0.0%	1	25.0%	1	25.0%	0	0.0%	4	26.7%
Introduction to a major, discipline, or career path	0	0.0%	4	36.4%	1	12.5%	2	33.3%	1	33.3%	0	0.0%	1	25.0%	2	50.0%	0	0.0%	4	26.7%
Introduction to college-level academic expectations	0	0.0%	2	18.2%	1	12.5%	1	16.7%	0	0.0%	0	0.0%	1	25.0%	1	25.0%	0	0.0%	2	13.3%
Introduction to the liberal arts	0	0.0%	3	27.3%	1	12.5%	2	33.3%	1	33.3%	0	0.0%	1	25.0%	1	25.0%	0	0.0%	3	20.0%
Knowledge of institution or campus resources and services	1	25.0%	4	36.4%	3	37.5%	2	33.3%	0	0.0%	1	100.0%	2	50.0%	2	50.0%	0	0.0%	5	33.3%
Major exploration	0	0.0%	4	36.4%	1	12.5%	3	50.0%	1	33.3%	0	0.0%	1	25.0%	2	50.0%	0	0.0%	4	26.7%
Oral communication skills	0	0.0%	5	45.5%	0	0.0%	0	0.0%	3	100.0%	0	0.0%	1	25.0%	1	25.0%	0	0.0%	5	33.3%
Persistence, retention, or third-year return rates	2	50.0%	7	63.6%	5	62.5%	4	66.7%	2	66.7%	1	100.0%	2	50.0%	2	50.0%	2	66.7%	9	60.0%
Personal exploration or development	1	25.0%	5	45.5%	4	50.0%	2	33.3%	1	33.3%	0	0.0%	2	50.0%	3	75.0%	0	0.0%	6	40.0%
Project planning, teamwork, or management skills	0	0.0%	2	18.2%	1	12.5%	1	16.7%	0	0.0%	0	0.0%	1	25.0%	1	25.0%	0	0.0%	2	13.3%

Table continues on page 125

Table continued from page 124

Survey question/ responses	Institutional type				Institution control				Number of undergraduates enrolled										Total	
	Two-year		Four-year		Public		Private		Fewer than 1,000		1,001-2,500		2,501-5,000		5,001-10,000		More than 10,000			
	Freq.	%	Freq	%	Freq.	%	Freq.	%	Freq.	%	Freq.	%	Freq.	%	Freq.	%	Freq.	%	Freq.	%
Q57: Please identify the student learning outcomes you assessed (Select all that apply)																				
Social support networks (e.g., friendships)	0	0.0%	1	9.1%	1	12.5%	0	0.0%	0	0.0%	0	0.0%	0	0.0%	1	25.0%	0	0.0%	1	6.7%
Student-faculty interaction	0	0.0%	3	27.3%	1	12.5%	2	33.3%	1	33.3%	0	0.0%	1	25.0%	1	25.0%	0	0.0%	3	20.0%
Writing skills	0	0.0%	6	54.5%	2	25.0%	3	50.0%	3	100.0%	0	0.0%	1	25.0%	2	50.0%	0	0.0%	6	40.0%
Other	1	25.0%	0	0.0%	1	12.5%	0	0.0%	0	0.0%	1	100.0%	0	0.0%	0	0.0%	0	0.0%	1	6.7%
Total	4	100.0%	11	100.0%	8	100.0%	6	100.0%	3	100.0%	1	100.0%	4	100.0%	4	100.0%	3	100.0%	15	100.0%
Q58: Please identify the national survey(s) you used: (Select all that apply)																				
College Student Experiences Questionnaire (CSEQ)	0	0.0%	1	14.3%	0	0.0%	1	16.7%	0	0.0%	1	25.0%	0	0.0%	0	0.0%	0	-	1	9.1%
Collegiate Learning Assessment (CLA)	1	25.0%	0	0.0%	1	20.0%	0	0.0%	0	0.0%	1	25.0%	0	0.0%	0	0.0%	0	-	1	9.1%
Community College Survey of Student Engagement (CCSSE)	4	100.0%	0	0.0%	4	80.0%	0	0.0%	0	0.0%	2	50.0%	2	40.0%	0	0.0%	0	-	4	36.4%
Diverse Learning Environments Study (DLE; Administered by HERI at UCLA)	0	0.0%	0	0.0%	0	0.0%	0	0.0%	0	0.0%	0	0.0%	0	0.0%	0	0.0%	0	-	0	0.0%
Faculty Survey of Student Engagement (FSSE)	1	25.0%	1	14.3%	1	20.0%	1	16.7%	0	0.0%	0	0.0%	2	40.0%	0	0.0%	0	-	2	18.2%
Individual Developmental and Educational Assessment (IDEA)	0	0.0%	0	0.0%	0	0.0%	0	0.0%	0	0.0%	0	0.0%	0	0.0%	0	0.0%	0	-	0	0.0%

Table continues on page 126

Table continued from page 125

Survey question/responses	Institutional type				Institution control				Number of undergraduates enrolled										Total	
	Two-year		Four-year		Public		Private		Fewer than 1,000		1,001-2,500		2,501-5,000		5,001-10,000		More than 10,000			
	Freq.	%	Freq	%	Freq.	%	Freq.	%	Freq.	%	Freq.	%	Freq.	%	Freq.	%	Freq.	%	Freq.	%
Q58: Please identify the national survey(s) you used: (Select all that apply)																				
National Survey of Student Engagement (NSSE)	0	0.0%	6	85.7%	1	20.0%	5	83.3%	1	100.0%	1	25.0%	3	60.0%	1	100.0%	0	-	6	54.5%
Second-Year Student Assessment (Noel-Levitz)	0	0.0%	1	14.3%	1	20.0%	0	0.0%	0	0.0%	0	0.0%	0	0.0%	1	100.0%	0	-	1	9.1%
Sophomore Experiences Survey (www.thrivingincollege.org)	0	0.0%	1	14.3%	0	0.0%	1	16.7%	0	0.0%	1	25.0%	0	0.0%	0	0.0%	0	-	1	9.1%
Student Satisfaction Inventory (SSI)	1	25.0%	1	14.3%	1	20.0%	1	16.7%	0	0.0%	0	0.0%	2	40.0%	0	0.0%	0	-	2	18.2%
Other	1	25.0%	2	28.6%	2	40.0%	1	16.7%	0	0.0%	2	50.0%	0	0.0%	1	100.0%	0	-	3	27.3%
Total	4	100.0%	7	100.0%	5	100.0%	6	100.0%	1	100.0%	4	100.0%	5	100.0%	1	100.0%	0	-	11	100.0%
Q59: If your institution does not have a sophomore initiative, indicate the reason(s) why: (Select all that apply)																				
Lack of expertise	2	6.1%	12	10.3%	6	7.3%	7	11.1%	4	14.8%	4	12.5%	2	5.7%	3	9.7%	1	4.2%	14	9.4%
Lack of funding	8	24.2%	42	36.2%	28	34.1%	20	31.7%	9	33.3%	11	34.4%	11	31.4%	11	35.5%	8	33.3%	50	33.6%
Lack of staff or faculty buy-in	3	9.1%	18	15.5%	10	12.2%	10	15.9%	7	25.9%	6	18.8%	3	8.6%	4	12.9%	1	4.2%	21	14.1%
Limited time	11	33.3%	35	30.2%	25	30.5%	19	30.2%	8	29.6%	11	34.4%	10	28.6%	10	32.3%	7	29.2%	46	30.9%
Not an institutional priority	10	30.3%	30	25.9%	21	25.6%	18	28.6%	7	25.9%	7	21.9%	12	34.3%	8	25.8%	6	25.0%	40	26.8%
Other	13	39.4%	54	46.6%	38	46.3%	26	41.3%	12	44.4%	16	50.0%	11	31.4%	15	48.4%	13	54.2%	67	45.0%
Total	33	100.0%	116	100.0%	82	100.0%	63	100.0%	27	100.0%	32	100.0%	35	100.0%	31	100.0%	24	100.0%	149	100.0%

Table continues on page 127

Table continued from page 126

Survey question/ responses	Institutional type				Institution control				Number of undergraduates enrolled										Total	
	Two-year		Four-year		Public		Private		Fewer than 1,000		1,001-2,500		2,501-5,000		5,001-10,000		More than 10,000			
	Freq.	%	Freq.	%	Freq.	%	Freq.	%	Freq.	%	Freq.	%	Freq.	%	Freq.	%	Freq.	%	Freq.	%
Q60. Has your institution had initiatives specifically or intentionally geared toward sophomore students in the past five years?																				
Yes	5	15.2%	14	12.1%	12	14.6%	6	9.5%	1	3.7%	3	9.4%	4	11.4%	4	12.9%	7	29.2%	19	12.8%
No	26	78.8%	89	76.7%	60	73.2%	52	82.5%	23	85.2%	24	75.0%	30	85.7%	21	67.7%	17	70.8%	115	77.2%
I don't know	2	6.1%	13	11.2%	10	12.2%	5	7.9%	3	11.1%	5	15.6%	1	2.9%	6	19.4%	0	0.0%	15	10.1%
Total	33	100.0%	116	100.0%	82	100.0%	63	100.0%	27	100.0%	32	100.0%	35	100.0%	31	100.0%	24	100.0%	149	100.0%
Q61: What were the sophomore-year initiatives? (Select all that apply)																				
Academic advising	3	60.0%	4	28.6%	7	58.3%	0	0.0%	0	0.0%	0	0.0%	2	50.0%	1	25.0%	4	57.1%	7	36.8%
Academic coaching or mentoring	2	40.0%	2	14.3%	3	25.0%	1	16.7%	0	0.0%	0	0.0%	2	50.0%	0	0.0%	2	28.6%	4	21.1%
Back-to-school events	0	0.0%	2	14.3%	0	0.0%	2	33.3%	0	0.0%	0	0.0%	1	25.0%	1	25.0%	0	0.0%	2	10.5%
Campus-based event (e.g., common reading experiences, dinners, fairs)	0	0.0%	1	7.1%	0	0.0%	1	16.7%	0	0.0%	0	0.0%	1	25.0%	0	0.0%	0	0.0%	1	5.3%
Career exploration	2	40.0%	5	35.7%	4	33.3%	2	33.3%	1	100.0%	1	33.3%	1	25.0%	2	50.0%	2	28.6%	7	36.8%
Career planning	2	40.0%	4	28.6%	4	33.3%	1	16.7%	1	100.0%	0	0.0%	1	25.0%	1	25.0%	3	42.9%	6	31.6%
Communication or publications (e.g., social media, newsletter, emails, brochures)	1	20.0%	0	0.0%	1	8.3%	0	0.0%	0	0.0%	0	0.0%	0	0.0%	0	0.0%	1	14.3%	1	5.3%
Course-specific support for classes with high D/F/W rates	0	0.0%	0	0.0%	0	0.0%	0	0.0%	0	0.0%	0	0.0%	0	0.0%	0	0.0%	0	0.0%	0	0.0%

Table continues on page 128

Table continued from page 127

Survey question/ responses	Institutional type				Institution control				Number of undergraduates enrolled										Total	
	Two-year		Four-year		Public		Private		Fewer than 1,000		1,001-2,500		2,501-5,000		5,001-10,000		More than 10,000			
	Freq.	%	Freq.	%	Freq.	%	Freq.	%	Freq.	%	Freq.	%	Freq.	%	Freq.	%	Freq.	%	Freq.	%
Q61: What were the sophomore-year initiatives? (Select all that apply)																				
Credit-bearing course (e.g., sophomore seminar)	0	0.0%	2	14.3%	1	8.3%	1	16.7%	0	0.0%	0	0.0%	1	25.0%	1	25.0%	0	0.0%	2	10.5%
Cultural enrichment activities	0	0.0%	0	0.0%	0	0.0%	0	0.0%	0	0.0%	0	0.0%	0	0.0%	0	0.0%	0	0.0%	0	0.0%
Early alert systems	1	20.0%	4	28.6%	3	25.0%	2	33.3%	0	0.0%	0	0.0%	2	50.0%	1	25.0%	2	28.6%	5	26.3%
Faculty or staff mentors	0	0.0%	0	0.0%	0	0.0%	0	0.0%	0	0.0%	0	0.0%	0	0.0%	0	0.0%	0	0.0%	0	0.0%
Financial aid	0	0.0%	1	7.1%	1	8.3%	0	0.0%	0	0.0%	0	0.0%	0	0.0%	0	0.0%	1	14.3%	1	5.3%
Internships or co-ops	0	0.0%	1	7.1%	1	8.3%	0	0.0%	0	0.0%	0	0.0%	0	0.0%	0	0.0%	1	14.3%	1	5.3%
Leadership development	0	0.0%	1	7.1%	1	8.3%	0	0.0%	0	0.0%	0	0.0%	0	0.0%	0	0.0%	1	14.3%	1	5.3%
Learning communities	0	0.0%	1	7.1%	1	8.3%	0	0.0%	0	0.0%	0	0.0%	0	0.0%	0	0.0%	1	14.3%	1	5.3%
Major exploration and selection	0	0.0%	2	14.3%	2	16.7%	0	0.0%	0	0.0%	0	0.0%	0	0.0%	2	50.0%	0	0.0%	2	10.5%
Off-campus event (e.g., retreat, outdoor adventure)	0	0.0%	0	0.0%	0	0.0%	0	0.0%	0	0.0%	0	0.0%	0	0.0%	0	0.0%	0	0.0%	0	0.0%
Opportunities to co-teach or assist in teaching a class	0	0.0%	2	14.3%	0	0.0%	2	33.3%	0	0.0%	1	33.3%	0	0.0%	1	25.0%	0	0.0%	2	10.5%
Peer mentoring by sophomores	1	20.0%	2	14.3%	1	8.3%	2	33.3%	0	0.0%	1	33.3%	0	0.0%	1	25.0%	1	14.3%	3	15.8%
Peer mentors for sophomores	0	0.0%	0	0.0%	0	0.0%	0	0.0%	0	0.0%	0	0.0%	0	0.0%	0	0.0%	0	0.0%	0	0.0%
Practica or other supervised practice experiences	0	0.0%	0	0.0%	0	0.0%	0	0.0%	0	0.0%	0	0.0%	0	0.0%	0	0.0%	0	0.0%	0	0.0%

Table continues on page 129

Table continued from page 128

Survey question/ responses	Institutional type				Institution control				Number of undergraduates enrolled										Total	
	Two-year		Four-year		Public		Private		Fewer than 1,000		1,001-2,500		2,501-5,000		5,001-10,000		More than 10,000			
	Freq.	%	Freq.	%	Freq.	%	Freq.	%	Freq.	%	Freq.	%	Freq.	%	Freq.	%	Freq.	%	Freq.	%
Q61: What were the sophomore-year initiatives? (Select all that apply)																				
Residence life - sophomore live on-campus requirement	0	0.0%	2	14.3%	0	0.0%	2	33.3%	0	0.0%	1	33.3%	1	25.0%	0	0.0%	0	0.0%	2	10.5%
Residence life - sophomore-specific living learning community	0	0.0%	0	0.0%	0	0.0%	0	0.0%	0	0.0%	0	0.0%	0	0.0%	0	0.0%	0	0.0%	0	0.0%
Residence life- sophomore-specific residential curriculum	0	0.0%	1	7.1%	0	0.0%	1	16.7%	0	0.0%	0	0.0%	0	0.0%	1	25.0%	0	0.0%	1	5.3%
Service-learning or community service	1	20.0%	2	14.3%	3	25.0%	0	0.0%	0	0.0%	0	0.0%	1	25.0%	0	0.0%	2	28.6%	3	15.8%
Student government	0	0.0%	1	7.1%	0	0.0%	1	16.7%	0	0.0%	1	33.3%	0	0.0%	0	0.0%	0	0.0%	1	5.3%
Study abroad	0	0.0%	2	14.3%	2	16.7%	0	0.0%	0	0.0%	0	0.0%	0	0.0%	0	0.0%	2	28.6%	2	10.5%
Undergraduate research	1	20.0%	3	21.4%	4	33.3%	0	0.0%	0	0.0%	0	0.0%	0	0.0%	0	0.0%	4	57.1%	4	21.1%
Other	1	20.0%	5	35.7%	4	33.3%	2	33.3%	0	0.0%	2	66.7%	0	0.0%	1	25.0%	3	42.9%	6	31.6%
Total	5	100.0%	14	100.0%	12	100.0%	6	100.0%	1	100.0%	3	100.0%	4	100.0%	4	100.0%	7	100.0%	19	100.0%
Q62. Is your institution considering or developing any future initiatives specifically or intentionally geared toward sophomore students?																				
Yes	12	36.4%	74	63.8%	50	61.0%	35	55.6%	11	40.7%	18	56.3%	19	54.3%	20	64.5%	18	75.0%	86	57.7%
No	16	48.5%	17	14.7%	19	23.2%	11	17.5%	8	29.6%	6	18.8%	8	22.9%	6	19.4%	5	20.8%	33	22.1%
I don't know	5	15.2%	25	21.6%	13	15.9%	17	27.0%	8	29.6%	8	25.0%	8	22.9%	5	16.1%	1	4.2%	30	20.1%
Total	33	100.0%	116	100.0%	82	100.0%	63	100.0%	27	100.0%	32	100.0%	35	100.0%	31	100.0%	24	100.0%	149	100.0%

Table continues on page 130

Table continued from page 129

Q63: Please indicate which of the following future sophomore initiative(s) your institution is considering or developing: (Select all that apply)

Survey question/ responses	Institutional type				Institution control				Number of undergraduates enrolled										Total	
	Two-year		Four-year		Public		Private		Fewer than 1,000		1,001-2,500		2,501-5,000		5,001-10,000		More than 10,000			
	Freq.	%	Freq.	%	Freq.	%	Freq.	%	Freq.	%	Freq.	%	Freq.	%	Freq.	%	Freq.	%	Freq.	%
Academic advising	8	66.7%	37	51.4%	24	49.0%	20	58.8%	5	50.0%	9	50.0%	15	78.9%	7	36.8%	9	50.0%	45	53.6%
Academic coaching or mentoring	6	50.0%	32	44.4%	22	44.9%	15	44.1%	5	50.0%	5	27.8%	9	47.4%	8	42.1%	11	61.1%	38	45.2%
Back-to-school events	2	16.7%	28	38.9%	16	32.7%	14	41.2%	3	30.0%	5	27.8%	9	47.4%	6	31.6%	7	38.9%	30	35.7%
Campus-based event (e.g., common reading experiences, dinners, fairs)	6	50.0%	20	27.8%	10	20.4%	15	44.1%	3	30.0%	7	38.9%	9	47.4%	3	15.8%	4	22.2%	26	31.0%
Career exploration	6	50.0%	40	55.6%	25	51.0%	20	58.8%	4	40.0%	11	61.1%	13	68.4%	9	47.4%	9	50.0%	46	54.8%
Career planning	11	91.7%	41	56.9%	30	61.2%	21	61.8%	8	80.0%	11	61.1%	13	68.4%	9	47.4%	11	61.1%	52	61.9%
Communication or publications (e.g., social media, newsletter, emails, brochures)	2	16.7%	11	15.3%	7	14.3%	5	14.7%	1	10.0%	3	16.7%	2	10.5%	3	15.8%	4	22.2%	13	15.5%
Course-specific support for classes with high D/F/W rates	5	41.7%	18	25.0%	13	26.5%	10	29.4%	3	30.0%	4	22.2%	7	36.8%	4	21.1%	5	27.8%	23	27.4%
Credit-bearing course (e.g., sophomore seminar)	0	0.0%	9	12.5%	6	12.2%	3	8.8%	0	0.0%	4	22.2%	1	5.3%	3	15.8%	1	5.6%	9	10.7%
Cultural enrichment activities	5	41.7%	7	9.7%	8	16.3%	4	11.8%	2	20.0%	3	16.7%	3	15.8%	3	15.8%	1	5.6%	12	14.3%
Early alert systems	8	66.7%	33	45.8%	26	53.1%	15	44.1%	3	30.0%	9	50.0%	14	73.7%	9	47.4%	6	33.3%	41	48.8%
Faculty or staff mentors	5	41.7%	16	22.2%	11	22.4%	10	29.4%	3	30.0%	4	22.2%	6	31.6%	5	26.3%	3	16.7%	21	25.0%

Table continues on page 131

Table continued from page 130

Q63: Please indicate which of the following future sophomore initiative(s) your institution is considering or developing: (Select all that apply)

Survey question/ responses	Institutional type				Institution control				Number of undergraduates enrolled										Total	
	Two-year		Four-year		Public		Private		Fewer than 1,000		1,001-2,500		2,501-5,000		5,001-10,000		More than 10,000			
	Freq.	%	Freq.	%	Freq.	%	Freq.	%	Freq.	%	Freq.	%	Freq.	%	Freq.	%	Freq.	%	Freq.	%
Financial aid	5	41.7%	14	19.4%	14	28.6%	5	14.7%	2	20.0%	4	22.2%	2	10.5%	6	31.6%	5	27.8%	19	22.6%
Internships or co-ops	7	58.3%	21	29.2%	18	36.7%	10	29.4%	3	30.0%	6	33.3%	7	36.8%	7	36.8%	5	27.8%	28	33.3%
Leadership development	6	50.0%	29	40.3%	20	40.8%	14	41.2%	5	50.0%	10	55.6%	5	26.3%	8	42.1%	7	38.9%	35	41.7%
Learning communities	1	8.3%	6	8.3%	5	10.2%	2	5.9%	1	10.0%	0	0.0%	1	5.3%	3	15.8%	2	11.1%	7	8.3%
Major exploration and selection	3	25.0%	17	23.6%	12	24.5%	8	23.5%	1	10.0%	5	27.8%	5	26.3%	4	21.1%	5	27.8%	20	23.8%
Off-campus event (e.g., retreat, outdoor adventure)	1	8.3%	6	8.3%	3	6.1%	4	11.8%	1	10.0%	2	11.1%	1	5.3%	2	10.5%	1	5.6%	7	8.3%
Opportunities to co-teach or assist in teaching a class	1	8.3%	6	8.3%	3	6.1%	4	11.8%	1	10.0%	2	11.1%	1	5.3%	1	5.3%	2	11.1%	7	8.3%
Peer mentoring by sophomores	5	41.7%	20	27.8%	16	32.7%	9	26.5%	1	10.0%	8	44.4%	7	36.8%	2	10.5%	7	38.9%	25	29.8%
Peer mentors for sophomores	2	16.7%	18	25.0%	10	20.4%	10	29.4%	2	20.0%	5	27.8%	7	36.8%	2	10.5%	4	22.2%	20	23.8%
Practica or other supervised practice experiences	3	25.0%	5	6.9%	4	8.2%	4	11.8%	1	10.0%	2	11.1%	3	15.8%	1	5.3%	1	5.6%	8	9.5%
Residence life - sophomore live on-campus requirement	0	0.0%	8	11.1%	5	10.2%	3	8.8%	0	0.0%	1	5.6%	3	15.8%	2	10.5%	2	11.1%	8	9.5%
Residence life - sophomore-specific living learning community	1	8.3%	10	13.9%	7	14.3%	4	11.8%	1	10.0%	1	5.6%	2	10.5%	4	21.1%	3	16.7%	11	13.1%

Table continues on page 132

Table continued from page 131

Q63: Please indicate which of the following future sophomore initiative(s) your institution is considering or developing: (Select all that apply)

| Survey question/ responses | Institutional type | | | | | | Institution control | | | | Number of undergraduates enrolled | | | | | | | | | | | Total | |
| | Two-year | | Four-year | | Public | | Private | | Fewer than 1,000 | | 1,001-2,500 | | 2,501-5,000 | | 5,001-10,000 | | More than 10,000 | | | |
	Freq.	%	Freq	%	Freq.	%	Freq.	%	Freq.	%	Freq.	%	Freq.	%	Freq.	%	Freq.	%	Freq.	%
Residence life-sophomore-specific residential curriculum	0	0.0%	5	6.9%	3	6.1%	2	5.9%	0	0.0%	0	0.0%	2	10.5%	1	5.3%	2	11.1%	5	6.0%
Service-learning or community service	6	50.0%	19	26.4%	11	22.4%	13	38.2%	4	40.0%	7	38.9%	4	21.1%	4	21.1%	6	33.3%	25	29.8%
Student government	3	25.0%	5	6.9%	4	8.2%	4	11.8%	2	20.0%	3	16.7%	0	0.0%	2	10.5%	1	5.6%	8	9.5%
Study abroad	2	16.7%	17	23.6%	9	18.4%	10	29.4%	2	20.0%	5	27.8%	6	31.6%	3	15.8%	3	16.7%	19	22.6%
Undergraduate research	1	8.3%	20	27.8%	11	22.4%	10	29.4%	3	30.0%	6	33.3%	4	21.1%	5	26.3%	3	16.7%	21	25.0%
Other	0	0.0%	4	5.6%	3	6.1%	1	2.9%	1	10.0%	0	0.0%	1	5.3%	1	5.3%	1	5.6%	4	4.8%
Total	12	100.0%	72	100.0%	49	100.0%	34	100.0%	10	100.0%	18	100.0%	19	100.0%	19	100.0%	18	100.0%	84	100.0%

References

American Association of Community Colleges. (2021). *AACC pathways project*. Retrieved from https://www.aacc.nche.edu/programs/aacc-pathways-project/

Ash, A., & Schreiner, L. A. (2016). Pathways to success in students of color on Christian campuses: The role of institutional integrity and sense of community. *Christian Higher Education, 15*(1–2), 38–61.

Barefoot, B. O., Gardner, J. N., Cutright, M., Morris, L. V., Schroeder, C. C., Schwartz, S. W., Siegel, M. J., & Swing, R. L. (2005). *Achieving and sustaining institutional excellence for the first year of college*. Jossey-Bass.

Blekic, M., Carpenter, R., & Cao, Y. (2020). Continuing and transfer students: Exploring retention and second-year success. *Journal of College Student Retention: Research, Theory & Practice, 22*(1), 71–98.

Bordes-Edgar, V., Arredondo, P., Kurpius, S. R., & Rund, J. (2011). A longitudinal analysis of Latina/o students' academic persistence. *Journal of Hispanic Higher Education, 10,* 358– 368. https://doi.org/10.1177/1538192711423318

Boyer Commission on Educating Undergraduates in the Research University. (1998). *Reinventing undergraduate education: A blueprint for America's research universities*. Carnegie Foundation for the Advancement of Teaching.

Center for Community College Student Engagement. (2014). *Aspirations to achievement: Men of color and community colleges* (A special report from the Center for Community College Student Engagement). Program in Higher Education Leadership, The University of Texas at Austin.

Center for Community College Student Engagement. (2017). *Even one semester: Full-time enrollment and student success*. The University of Texas at Austin, College of Education, Department of Educational Administration, Program in Higher Education Leadership.

Consortium for Student Retention Data Exchange. (2015). *2014–15 CSRDE retention report: The retention and graduation rates of entering baccalaureate degree-seeking freshman cohorts from fall 2004 through fall 2013 in 345 colleges and universities*.

Crisp, G. (2010). The impact of mentoring on the success of community college students. *The Review of Higher Education, 34*(1), 39–60.

Gahagan, J. (2010). Institutional policies that impact sophomore success. *New Directions for Higher Education, 2018*(183), 85–95. http://doi.org/10.1002/he.20295

Gay, G. (2010). *Culturally responsive teaching* (2nd ed.). Teachers College Press.

Golden, A. E. (2011). *First generation Latina persistence group mentoring and sophomore success* (Publication No. 3482161) [Doctoral dissertation, Arizona State University]. ProQuest Dissertations and Theses Global.

Goldrick-Rab, S. (2010). Challenges and opportunities for improving community college student success. *Review of Educational Research, 80*(3), 437–469.

Gordon, V. N. (1998). Career decidedness types: A literature review. *The Career Development Quarterly, 46*(4), 386–403.

Gordon, V. N. (2010). Academic advising: Helping sophomores succeed. In M. S. Hunter, B. F. Tobolowsky, J. N. Gardner, S. E. Evenbeck, J. A. Pattengale, M. A. Schaller, & L. A. Schreiner (Eds.), *Helping sophomores succeed: Understanding and improving the second-year experience* (pp. 83–98). Jossey-Bass.

Graunke, S. S., & Woosley, S. A. (2005). An exploration of the factors that affect the academic success of college sophomores. *College Student Journal, 39*(2), 367–376.

Herrera, A., & Jain, D. (2013). Building a transfer-receptive culture at four-year institutions. *New Directions for Higher Education, 162,* 51–59. https://doi.org/10.1002/he.20056

HigherEd Direct. (2019). *Higher education directory.* https://hepinc.com/product/highered-direct-license-1-2-subscriptions/

Hunter, M. S., Tobolowsky, B. F., Gardner, J. N., Evenbeck, S. E., Pattengale, J. A., Schaller, M., & Schreiner, L. A. (Eds.). (2010). *Helping sophomores succeed: Understanding and improving the second-year experience.* Jossey-Bass.

Hunter, M. S., Tobolowsky, B. F., Gardner, J. N., Evenbeck, S. E., Pattengale, J. A., Schaller, M., & Schreiner, L. A. (2009). *Helping sophomores succeed: Understanding and improving the second year experience.* John Wiley & Sons.

Ishitani, T. T. (2016). Time-varying effects of academic and social integration on student persistence for first and second years in college: National data approach. *Journal of College Student Retention: Research, Theory & Practice, 18*(3), 263–286.

Johnson, I. Y., & Muse, W. B. (2012). Student swirl at a single institution: The role of timing and student characteristics. *Research in Higher Education, 53,* 152–181.

Kim, Y. K. (2010). Racially different patterns of student–faculty interaction: A focus on levels, effects, and causal directions. *Journal of the Professoriate, 3*(2), 161–189.

Kim, Y. K., & Sax, L. J. (2017). The impact of college students' interactions with faculty: A review of general and conditional effects. In M. B. Paulsen (Ed.), *Higher education: Handbook of theory and research* (Vol. 32, pp. 85–139). Springer.

Kuh, G. D. (2008). *High-impact educational practices: What they are, who has access to them, and why they matter.* Association of American Colleges & Universities.

Kuh, G. D. (2013). Promise in action: Examples of institutional effectiveness. In D. Kalsbeek (Ed.), *Reframing retention strategy for institutional improvement* (New Directions for Higher Education, No. 161). Jossey-Bass. https://doi.org/10.1002/he.20048

Kuh, G. D., Kinzie, J., Schuh, J. H., & Whitt, E. J. (2005). *Student success in college: Creating conditions that matter.* Jossey-Bass.

Lee, J. A. (2018). Affirmation, support, and advocacy: Critical race theory and academic advising. *The Journal of the National Academic Advising Association, 38*(1), 77–87.

Lundberg, C. A., & Schreiner, L. A. (2004). Quality and frequency of faculty–student interaction as predictors of learning: An analysis by student race/ethnicity. *Journal of College Student Development, 45*(5), 549–565. https://doi.org/10.1353/csd.2004.0061

Mangan, K. (2018, April 30). These 2-year and 4-year college partnerships keep students from falling through the cracks. *The Chronicle of Higher Education.* https://www.chronicle.com/article/these-2-year-and-4-year-college-partnerships-keep-students-from-falling-through-the-cracks/

Maslow, A. H. (1943). A theory of human motivation. *Psychological Review, 50*(4), 370–396.

Mobelini, D. C. (2013). Community colleges: Partnerships in higher education. *Community College Journal of Research and Practice, 37*(8), 629–635. https://doi.org/10.1080/10668921003723151

National Student Clearinghouse. (2019). *First-year persistence and retention for fall 2017 cohort.* Retrieved from https://nscresearchcenter.org/wp-content/uploads/SnapshotReport35.pdf

Peteren, A. (2019). *Exploring Black student success with a mixed methods investigation of retention in the second year of college* [Unpublished doctoral dissertation]. California State University, San Marcos.

Provencher, A., & Kassel, R. (2019). High-impact practices and sophomore retention: Examining the effects of selection bias. *Journal of College Student Retention: Research, Theory & Practice, 21*(2), 221–241.

Reason, R. D. (2009). An examination of persistence research through the lens of a comprehensive conceptual framework. *Journal of College Student Development 50*(6), 659–682. https://doi.org/10.1353/csd.0.0098.

Schaller, M. A. (2010). Understanding the impact of the second year of college. In M. S. Hunter, B. F. Tobolowsky, J. N. Gardner, S. E. Evenbeck, J. A. Pattengale, M. A. Schaller, & L. A. Schreiner (Eds.), *Helping sophomores succeed: Understanding and improving the second-year experience* (pp. 13–29). Jossey-Bass.

Schreiner, L. A. (2018). Thriving in the second year of college: Pathways to success. In L. A. Schreiner (Ed.), *Sophomore success: Making the most of the second year* (New Directions for Higher Education, No. 183, pp. 9–21). Wiley. https://doi.org/10.1002/he.20289

Schreiner, L. A., & Pattengale, J. (Eds.). (2000). *Visible solutions for invisible students: Helping sophomores succeed* (Monograph No. 31). University of South Carolina, National Resource Center for The First-Year Experience & Students in Transition.

Schreiner, L. A., & Tobolowsky, B. F. (2018). The role of faculty in sophomore success. In L. A. Schreiner (Ed.), *Sophomore success: Making the most of the second year* (New Directions for Higher Education, No. 183, pp. 59–70). Wiley. https://doi.org/10.1002/he.20293

Schreiner, L. A., Louis, M. C., & Nelson, D. D. (Eds.). (2020). *Thriving in transitions: A research-based approach to college student success* (2nd ed.). University of South Carolina, National Resource Center for The First-Year Experience & Students in Transition.

Schreiner, L. A., Schaller, M. A., & Young, D. G. (2018). Future directions for enhancing sophomore success. In L. A. Schreiner (Ed.), *Sophomore success: Making the most of the second year* (New Directions for Higher Education, No. 183, pp. 109–112). Wiley.

Scott, I. (2012). First-year experience as terrain of failure or platform for development? Critical choices for higher education. In B. Leibowitz, A. van der Merwe, & S. van Schalkwyk (Eds.), *Focus on first-year success: Perspectives emerging from South Africa and beyond*. Sun Press.

Skipper, T. L. (Ed.). (2019). *Aligning institutional support for student success: Case studies of sophomore-year initiatives* (Research Report No. 10). University of South Carolina, National Resource Center for The First-Year Experience & Students in Transition.

Taylor, J. L., & Jain, D. (2017). The multiple dimensions of transfer: Examining the transfer function in American higher education. *Community College Review, 45*(4), 273–293. https://doi.org/10.1177/0091552117725177

Tovar, E. (2015). The role of faculty, counselors, and support programs on Latino/a community college students' success and intent to persist. *Community College Review, 43*(1), 46–71.

Truong, S. (2021, May 13). *Student stories: The journey from community college*. Inside Higher Ed. https://www.insidehighered.com/blogs/tackling-transfer/student-stories-journey-community-college#.YJz1Phd0414.twitter

U.S. Department of Education, National Center for Education Statistics, Integrated Postsecondary System (IPEDS). (2020). *Institutional characteristics surveys* [Data files and dictionaries]. https://nces.ed.gov/ipeds/use-the-data

Virginia Commonwealth University. (2021). *Pathways to VCU*. https://transfer.vcu.edu/partnerships-and-agreements/pathways-to-vcu/

Yosso, T. J. (2005). Whose culture has capital? A critical race theory discussion of community cultural wealth. *Race Ethnicity and Education, 8*(1), 69–91.

Young, D. G. (2016). The case for an integrated approach to transition programmes at South Africa's higher education institutions. *Journal of Student Affairs in Africa, 4*(1), 15–30.

Young, D. G., & Keup, J. R. (2019). *Cross-functional framework for first-year experiences*. Council for the Advancement of Standards in Higher Education.

Young, D. G., Schreiner, L. A., & MacIntosh, E. J. (2015). *Investigating sophomore student success: National Survey of Sophomore-Year Initiatives and the Sophomore Experience Survey, 2014* (Research Report No. 6). University of South Carolina, National Resource Center for The First-Year Experience and Students in Transition.

About the Authors

Dr. Catherine Hartman is a postdoctoral research associate at the National Resource Center for The First-Year Experience and Students in Transition. Catherine works with Center staff to carry out projects related to the Center's research agenda and grant-seeking activities. Her research focuses on community college student persistence and engagement, student transfer from community colleges to four-year schools, and community college leadership.

Dr. Dallin George Young is an assistant professor in College Student Affairs Administration (CSAA) and Student Affairs Leadership (SAL) at the University of Georgia. His research agenda includes using activity-based theoretical perspectives to interrogate student transitions into the academy; how graduate and professional students learn the rules, knowledge, and culture of their aspirational professional communities; and the impacts of educational structures on the success of these transitions, including investigating differential effects on student populations.